24.95

Politics of Masculinities:
Men in Movements

THE GENDER LENS SERIES IN SOCIOLOGY

Series Editors

Judith A. Howard
University of Washington

Barbara Risman
North Carolina State University

Mary Romero
Arizona State University

Joey Sprague
University of Kansas

Authors

Yen Le Espiritu, *Asian American Women and Men: Labor, Laws, and Love*

Judith A. Howard and Jocelyn Hollander, *Gendered Situations, Gendered Selves: A Gender Lens on Social Psychology*

Michael A. Messner, *Politics of Masculinities: Men in Movements*

Politics of Masculinities

Men in Movements

Michael A. Messner
University of Southern California

SAGE PUBLICATIONS
Thousand Oaks ■ London ■ New Delhi

For information, address to:

 SAGE Publications, Inc.
2455 Teller Road
Thousand Oaks, California 91320
E-mail: order@sagepub.com

SAGE Publications Ltd.
6 Bonhill Street
London EC2A 4PU
United Kingdom

SAGE Publications India Pvt. Ltd.
M-32 Market
Greater Kailash I
New Delhi 110 048 India

Printed in the United States of America

Library of Congress Cataloging-in-Publication Data

Messner, Michael A.
    Politics of masculinities: Men in movements/author, Michael A. Messner
        p. cm.—(Gender lens; vol. 3)
    Includes bibliographical references and index.
    ISBN 0-8039-5576-6 (cloth: acid-free paper).—ISBN 0-8039-5577-4
(pbk.: acid-free paper)
        1. Men's movement—United States. 2. Men—United States. 3. Sex role—
United States. 4. Masculinity (Psychology)—United States.
I. Title. II. Series.
HQ1090.3.M475 1997
305.32—dc20   96-35667

This book is printed on acid-free paper that meets
Environmental Protection Agency standards for recycled paper.

98 99 00 01 02 03 10 9 8 7 6 5 4 3 2

Acquiring Editor:	Peter Labella
Editorial Assistant:	Frances Borghi
Production Editor:	Diana E. Axelsen
Production Assistant:	Karen Wiley
Typesetter/Designer:	Marion Warren
Indexer:	Trish Wittenstein
Print Buyer:	Anna Chin

CONTENTS

For Miles and Sasha

It is now over 20 years since feminist sociologists identified gender as an important analytic dimension in sociology. In the intervening two decades, theory and research on gender have grown exponentially. With this series, we intend to further this scholarship, as well as ensure that theory and research on gender become fully integrated into the discipline as a whole.

Beth Hess and Myra Marx Ferree, in *Analyzing Gender* (1988), identified three stages in the study of women and men since 1970. Initially, the emphasis was on sex differences and the extent to which such differences might be based in biological properties of individuals. In the second stage, the focus shifted to individual-level sex roles and socialization, exposing gender as the product of specific social arrangements, although still conceptualizing it as an individual trait. The hallmark of the third stage is the recognition of the centrality of gender as an organizing principle in all social systems, including work, politics, everyday interaction, families, economic development, law, education, and a host of other social domains. As our understanding of gender has become more social, so has our awareness that gender is experienced and organized in race- and class-specific ways.

In the summer of 1992 the American Sociological Association (ASA) funded a small conference, organized by Barbara Risman and Joey Sprague, to discuss the evolution of gender in these distinctly sociological frameworks. The conference brought together a sampling of gender scholars working in a wide range of substantive areas with a diversity of methods to focus on gender as a principle of social organization. The discussions of the state of feminist scholarship made it clear that gender is pervasive in society and operates at multiple levels. Gender shapes identities and perception, interactional practices, and the very forms of social institutions, and it does so in race- and class-specific ways. If we did not see gender in social phenomena, we were not seeing clearly. The participants in this ASA-sponsored seminar recognized that although these developing ideas about gender were widely accepted by feminist sociologists and many others who study social inequalities, they were relatively unfamiliar to many who work within other sociological paradigms. This book series was conceived at that conference as a means to introduce these ideas to sociological colleagues and students and to help further develop gender scholarship.

As series editors, we feel it is time for gender scholars to speak to our colleagues and to the general education of students. There are many sociologists and scholars in other social sciences who want to incorporate scholarship on gender and its intersections with race, class, and sexuality in their teaching and research, but lack the tools to do so. For those who have not worked in this area, the prospect of the bibliographic research necessary to develop supplementary units, or to transform their own teaching and scholarship, is daunting. Moreover, the publications necessary to penetrate a curriculum resistant to change and encumbered by inertia have simply not been available. We conceptualize this book series as a way of meeting the needs of these scholars, and thereby also encouraging the development of the sociological understanding of gender by offering a "gender lens."

What do we mean by a "gender lens"? It means working to make gender visible in social phenomena, asking if, how, and why social processes, standards, and opportunities differ systematically for women and men. It also means recognizing that gender inequality is inextricably braided with other systems of inequity. Looking at the world through a gendered lens thus implies two seemingly contradictory tasks. First, it means unpacking the taken-for-granted assumptions about gender that pervade sociological research, and social life more generally. At the same time, looking through a gender lens means showing just how central assumptions about gender continue to be to the organization of the social world, regardless of their empirical reality. We show how our often unquestioned ideas about gender affect the worlds we see, the questions we ask, the answers we can envision. The **Gender Lens Series** is committed to social change directed toward eradicating these inequalities. Our goals are consistent with initiatives at colleges and universities across the United States that are encouraging the development of more diverse scholarship and teaching.

The books in the **Gender Lens Series** are aimed at different audiences and have been written for a variety of uses, from assigned readings in introductory undergraduate courses to graduate seminars, and as professional resources for our colleagues. The series includes several different styles of books that address these goals in distinct ways. We are excited about this series and anticipate that it will have an enduring impact on the direction of both pedagogy and scholarship in sociology and other related social sciences. We invite you, the reader, to join us in thinking through these difficult but exciting issues by offering feedback or developing your own project and proposing it to us for the series.

About This Volume

The current volume presents a gendered analysis of a social category for whom gender has been thought to be self-evident, yet has been anything but—men. Michael Messner builds upon the recent explosion of research on men and masculinity to offer a sociological framework for understanding men's organized responses to changes, challenges, and crises in the social organization of gender. He focuses on the political discourses and practices of social movements that are engaged with the politics of masculinity. He draws on recent research that illuminates boys' and men's relationships with and experiences in families, workplaces, and schools, as well as the recent debates about sexualities and violence.

Messner organizes the discussion around a unique model of social movements, a model he calls "the terrain of masculinity politics." He uses this model to analyze eight such movements, including men's liberationists, men's rights advocates, radical feminist men, social feminist men, men of color, gay male liberationists, Promise Keepers, and the mythopoetic men's movement. This analysis focuses on three factors: men's institutionalized privileges, the costs attached to adherence to narrow conceptions of masculinity, and differences and inequalities among men. Considering how each of these eight movements has variously emphasized or failed to attend to each of these three factors leads to a sophisticated understanding of how contemporary men have come to grapple with the meaning of manhood. In evaluating the extent to which these movements can serve as a locus for activity by men who seek to promote social justice, Messner argues that recent perspectives on gender introduced by feminist women of color offer the most promising position today from which to establish a progressive politics of masculinities.

We hope this book and others in the **Gender Lens Series** will help the reader develop his or her own gender lens to better and more accurately understand our social environments. As sociologists, we believe that an accurate understanding of inequality is a prerequisite for effective social change.

Judith A. Howard
Barbara Risman
Mary Romero
Joey Sprague
Gender Lens Series Editors

Not long ago, I was standing in line behind a woman and a man at the local car wash, waiting to pay the cashier. As the man, a thirtyish white guy wearing a tight tank top, paid his money, the female cashier asked him about the prominent Asian characters that were tattooed on his heavily muscled arm. "Is that Chinese?" she asked him. "No," he replied tersely, "it's Korean." She persisted in her curiosity: "What's it say?" He lifted the arm a bit and flexed: "It says, 'Fear No Man, Trust No Woman.' " An uncomfortable moment of silence passed as he got his change and left. Then, the next woman in line stepped forward to pay her money, and the cashier said to her, "That's pretty scary!" "I don't know," the other woman replied. "I think they *all* should come with warning labels."

At first, I thought about this scene only in terms of how women today are often so adept at poking fun not only at some men's hyper-masculine posturing but also at the very real danger of violence that all men potentially represent. But as I thought more about it, I began to think and wonder about what might have compelled this man to inscribe—apparently permanently—this depressing message on his arm. "Fear No Man, Trust No Woman." Imagine the isolation, loneliness, and alienation that must underlie such a slogan.

And I began to ponder the "No Fear" slogan that has appeared lately on the baseball caps, T-shirts, and bumper stickers of boys and young men, seemingly everywhere. It seems to me that you don't see hundreds of thousands of people massed in the streets chanting for peace unless you already have war. And you don't have a whole generation of young males publicly proclaiming that they have "No Fear" unless there's something actually scaring the crap out of them.

What are men so afraid of today? Most obviously, they are afraid of other men's violence. Young African American males in particular are falling prey to each other's violence in epidemic proportions, but young males from all social groups feel increasingly vulnerable today. Less obvious, but just as ominous, are young men's worries and fears of an uncertain future. As deindustrialization has eliminated tens of thousands of inner-city jobs, as structural unemployment has risen, and as government has become increasingly unable and unwilling to provide hope, a higher and higher proportion of young males today see that the image of the male family breadwinner is increasingly unattainable for them.

It's actually getting harder and harder for a young male to figure out how to *be* a man. But this is not necessarily a bad thing. Young men's current fears of other men and the continued erosion of the male breadwinner role might offer a historic opportunity for men—individually and collectively—to reject narrow, limiting, and destructive definitions of masculinity and, instead, to create a more humane, peaceful, and egalitarian definition of manhood. But standing in the way of that goal is a deeply internalized distrust of women. This distrust of women is reflected in many—though not all—of the "men's movements" that are the subject of this book. Although they are very different in some important ways, many of the men's movements that have sprung up in the 1980s and 1990s share a commitment to rebuilding and revaluing bonds among men, to overcoming men's fears of each other, and to pushing men to be responsible and peaceful fathers and husbands. This in itself represents an important and potentially positive groundswell among diverse groups of men. But many of these groups also share another more troubling characteristic: They clearly believe that for men to overcome their fears of other men, they must separate themselves from women. And this separation from women is spoken of in terms of men's "empowerment"—to reclaim their "natural" roles as leaders in families and communities.

Most troubling is that this talk of men's need for "empowerment" and the need to restore men to their "natural" and "God-given" positions as leaders is taking place largely within organizations that have defined themselves as male only. Thus, the developing discourse of these organizations tends to preclude serious dialogue with women and with women's organizations. The result, I fear, might be that as men organize to assuage their own fears, they collectively position women, especially feminists, as convenient scapegoats. In restoring men to their own "rightful place," they put women back in theirs. In the process, the impressive (though partial) gains made by the women's movement in the past 30 years are at risk of being turned back.

Men do need to acknowledge our fears and doubts, and we do need to talk with other men about these issues. But this needs to be done within the context of a respectful dialogue with women and with the acknowledgment that healing men's problems and fears cannot be accomplished by putting women down. Rather, as some of the more positive examples of "masculinity politics" in this book illustrate, it is through contributing to the empowerment of women that men will become more fully human.

This book is dedicated to my two young sons, Miles and Sasha. I hope that as they grow up, they will not live in a world that makes them believe that to feel safe, secure, and confident, they must "Fear no man; trust no woman." Instead, I want them to live in a world that encourages them to respect, trust, and love women and men as equal human beings. It is my hope that this book is one small contribution to moving us toward such a world.

ACKNOWLEDGMENTS

The ideas in this book stem from my nearly two decades of teaching, reading, thinking, and writing about men, masculinities, and gender relations, all at a time in history when the scholarly examination of these topics has expanded astronomically. There really is no way I can acknowledge or thank all of the students, teachers, and scholars who have influenced my thinking on these topics (though many are represented in my list of references at the end of the book). I have decided, then, to acknowledge here only the people who have made direct contributions to the development of the manuscript for this book.

As I began to research this book, there were some groups and organizations about which I knew very little. Both Jay Coakley and Becky Beal generously shared their thoughts and ongoing research on Promise Keepers with me. Their leads were especially important to the development of my thinking on this group. My understanding of the 1980s roots of Promise Keepers was aided by information that Hiram Davis shared with me. Michael Schwalbe is certainly the leading expert sociologist on the mythopoetic men's movement; I have benefited both from his published research and from discussions I have had with him. Though I've been a member of the National Organization for Men Against Sexism (NOMAS, formerly NOCM) since the early 1980s, Michael Kimmel's close involvement with the organization has expanded my insight into this group. And my discussion of the rise of the men's liberation movement was enriched when Barrie Thorne shared her early 1970s files with me. Peter Nardi's knowledge of gay and lesbian organizations has similarly stretched my knowledge of gender politics in gay and lesbian liberation.

As I began to develop the conceptual framework that forms the backbone of this book, my thoughts were aided by stimulating conver-

xvii

sations with Barrie Thorne and Jim McKay. Talks that I gave to faculty and student colloquia at Sonoma State University, the University of California, Santa Barbara, and the University of Kansas gave me valuable opportunities to try out some of the ideas in this book with supportive groups of scholars. And I was given critical and thought-provoking comments and suggestions on earlier versions of chapters, or, in some cases, the entire manuscript, by the following people: Bob Connell, Pierrette Hondagneu-Sotelo, Judy Howard, Michael Kimmel, Peter Nardi, Jim McKay, Don Sabo, Michael Schwalbe, and Cliff Staples. Yolanda Denise Nelms contributed her time and expertise in putting together the figures that appear in the text. The quality of the final product was considerably enhanced by the collective input of all of these people. Of course, the responsibility for any mistakes, blind spots, or inconsistencies in the argument is, in the final analysis, mine. Indeed, I should note that some of these readers disagreed with parts of what I have to say in the book.

Finally, I want to gratefully acknowledge the Gender Lens collective and especially Judy Howard, my Gender Lens editor, for her intelligent suggestions, her encouragement, and, especially, her patience. Thanks also to Peter Labella and Diana Axelsen at Sage for their supportive and professional work in shepherding this work from manuscript to book form. I am proud to have this book appear as part of a series of Gender Lens books that we hope will have an impact on making feminist research more central in sociology—and by extension, in the world.

CHAPTER 1

Men and Masculinities

> The closer we come to uncovering some form of exemplary
> masculinity, a masculinity which is solid and sure of itself, the
> clearer it becomes that masculinity is structured through
> contradiction: the more it asserts itself, the more it calls itself into
> question.
>
> —*Lynne Segal (1990, p. 123)*

In the past few years, the United States has discovered men. Television talk shows focus on "today's fathers" or on men's midlife crises; popular shows such as *Murphy Brown* and *Home Improvement* satirize some contemporary men's insecurities and stylistic fads. Meanwhile, real-life men have been responding to—and at times initiating—changes in the personal and social relations of gender. Consider the following developments:

■ Many born-again Christians are subtly redefining women's and men's "God-given roles" (Stacey, 1990), and conservative ministers are holding popular seminars on "the meaning of manhood." For instance, in 1995, over 600,000 Christian men, led by University of Colorado football coach Bill McCartney, packed several football stadiums throughout the United States to listen to sermons, sing, and pray about their roles as men. McCartney claims that by the year 2000, he will have enrolled 1 million men in his Promise Keepers organization, which aims to help Christian men reclaim the spiritual leadership in their families and communities.

■ Gay liberationists and profeminist men in organizations such as the National Organization of Men Against Sexism (NOMAS) are joining forces with feminist women to confront rape, sexual harassment, sexism, and homophobia on college campuses and in workplaces, the

1

media, and the political system (Clatterbaugh, 1990; Edwards, 1990; Shiffman, 1987).

■ "Men's rights" activists are angrily proclaiming that men are the true victims of prostitution, pornography, dating rituals, sexist media conventions, divorce settlements, false rape accusations, sexual harassment, and even domestic violence and are organizing to change laws they say are harmful to men (Baumli, 1985; Farrell, 1993).

■ In the past decade, thousands of men have attended the poet Robert Bly's "mythopoetic" men's weekends in the woods to ritually recover their lost manhood (Schwalbe, 1995a). Bly's 1990 book, *Iron John: A Book About Men,* sold over 500,000 hardcover copies and was the national nonfiction best-seller of the year. Other mythopoetic men's books, such as Sam Keen's (1991) *Fire in the Belly* and Robert Moore and Douglas Gillette's (1991) *King, Warrior, Magician, Lover,* also sold thousands of copies.

■ In October 1995, hundreds of thousands of African American men, led by Minister Louis Farrakhan and the Nation of Islam, joined the Million Man March in Washington, D.C., to pray for "atonement" and to express a collective commitment to restore men's sense of moral responsibility and leadership in crisis-torn families and communities. In the aftermath of the march, organizations such as the National Association for the Advancement of Colored People (NAACP) and Big Brothers reported a surge of membership by African American males.

Clearly, the question is not, Can men change? or Will men change? Men *are* changing, but not in any singular manner and not necessarily in the directions that feminist women would like. Some of these changes support feminism, some express a backlash against feminism, and others (such as Bly's retreat to an idealized tribal mythology of male homosociality) appear to be attempts to avoid feminist issues altogether. One thing is clear: Although these changes by men are not all feminist, the growing concern with the "problem of masculinity" takes place within a social context that has been partially transformed by feminism. Like it or not, men today must deal, on some level, with gender as a problematic construct rather than as a natural, taken-for-granted reality (Connell, 1993, 1995; Messner, 1993a).

How can we make sense of these myriad, often contradictory expressions of masculinity? This book builds on the recent explosion of research on men and masculinity to offer a sociological framework for understanding men's organized responses to changes, challenges, and crises in the social organization of gender. My focus will be on the political discourse and practice of various social movements that are engaged in the politics of masculinity. That is, I will examine what certain groups and organizations *say* about gender, as well as what they *do*. I will draw on recent research that illuminates boys' and men's relationships and experiences in families, workplaces, schools, and religion, as well as on the recent debates about sexuality and violence. The remainder of this chapter will be concerned with introducing the three themes and the model that form the basis for my examination of men and masculinities: men's institutionalized privileges, the costs of masculinity, and differences and inequalities among men. Although in this chapter I will employ anecdotes from my own life to introduce the three conceptual themes, I want to underline that they emerge from my reading of rapidly burgeoning social scientific literature on men and masculinities.

Institutionalized Privilege

In the early 1970s, when I was an undergraduate, I took a course on social inequality in which I was confronted with research that showed that women in the paid labor force were earning about $.59 to the male's dollar. Even women who were working in the same occupations as men, I learned, were earning substantially less than their male counterparts. These facts radically contradicted what I had been taught about the United States: that this is a country of equal opportunity in which merit is rewarded independent of race, religion, or sex. In a term paper for this course, I explored the reasons for gender inequities in the workforce and stated passionately in my conclusion that it was only fair for women to have equal rights with men. My professor liked the paper, and I felt proud that I had taken a "profeminist" position.

The following summer, I was back in my hometown, working at my regular summer job as a recreation worker in city parks. With the exception of two full-time supervisors, the summer staff consisted of about 15 temporary workers who were, like me, college students. Perhaps a dozen or so of these workers were women, and three of us were men, giving the appearance, perhaps, that this was a female-dominated job. But what had not occurred to me at the time, or struck me as unusual, was that all of the women had been given 20- or 30-hour per week assignments at smaller city parks, whereas each of the men had been assigned 40-hour weeks at the larger parks. What's more, when opportunities for overtime work arose, the supervisors invariably invited the men to do the work. So I regularly chalked up 42, perhaps even 46, hours of work each week. One week, at a staff meeting, a supervisor routinely invited me and another man to come to the recreation center to do some overtime work. Before we had a chance to say yes, we were interrupted by one of the women workers, who firmly stated, "I don't know why the guys always get the extra hours; we women can do that work as well as them. It doesn't really seem fair." I immediately felt threatened and defensive and broke the uncomfortable moment of silence in the room by whispering—far too loudly, as it turned out—to my male coworker, "Who the hell does she think she is, Gloria Steinem?" In response, the woman worker glared and pointed her finger at me: "Don't talk about something you don't know anything about, Mike!"

Immediately, it ran through my mind that I *did*, in fact, know *a lot* about this topic. Why, I had just written this wonderful paper about how women workers are paid less than men and had taken the position that this should change. Why, then, when faced with a concrete situation where I could put that knowledge and those principles to work had I taken a defensive, reactionary position? In retrospect, I can see that I had not yet learned the difference between taking an intellectual position on an issue and actually integrating principles into my life ("the personal is political," my feminist friends would later teach me). But more important, I had not yet come to grips with the reality that men—especially white, heterosexual, middle-class men like myself—tend to take for granted certain *institutional privileges*. In this case, because I was a man, I was "just naturally" afforded greater opportunities than my female coworkers. Yes, I had to work hard, but I worked no harder than did the women. Yet, to receive equal treatment, the women had to stand up for themselves and make public claims based on values of justice and equal opportunity. I just had to show up. What strikes me about this in retrospect is how easy it is for members of a privileged group to remain ignorant of the ways that the social structures of which we are a part grant us privileges, often at the expense of others.

Part of the goal of this book is to illustrate that, after nearly three decades of a resurgent women's movement and some significant gains for women in public life, this is still the case. The United States has never had a female president or vice president, and the U.S. Congress, Senate, Supreme Court, and military are still largely bastions of men's power.

Women are still not allowed to be ordained as Catholic priests, and nearly all other organized religions have men at the top of their hierarchies. Women's median annual incomes are still about two thirds of men's, and women workers are still disproportionately clustered in lower-pay, lower-status occupations (Blum, 1991; Reskin & Padavic, 1994; Reskin & Roos, 1990; Williams, 1993). And in families, women are still responsible for the vast majority of housework and child care, even when they are also in the paid labor force (Coltrane, 1989, 1996; Hochschild, 1989). This, then, is the first theme that will be emphasized throughout this book:

> *Men, as a group, enjoy institutional*
> *privileges at the expense of women, as a group.*

This is not to say that men's institutional power over women is total or unchanging. Rather, gender is a system of unequal—but shifting and at times contested—power relations between women and men (Connell, 1987). In the current historical moment, men's institutional privileges still persist, by and large, but they no longer can be entirely taken for granted. For the past three decades, women have organized to actively challenge unequal and unfair gender arrangements. This reality was brought home to me over 20 years ago quite dramatically by my female workmate.

The Costs of Masculinity

In 1977, a major support undergirding my world suddenly gave way when my father died. It just didn't seem fair: A nonsmoker, moderate social drinker, and former athlete only a few pounds overweight, he appeared to have lived a fairly healthy life. Seemingly vibrant at the age of 56, he was just too young to die. But within a few short months, cancer quickly dropped the man who, to our family, had always seemed like the Rock of Gibraltar. And maybe, I can now see, that was part of the problem. As a high school and college football player in the 1930s and 1940s, then in the navy in World War II, he had been taught that a real man ignores his own pain and pays whatever price is necessary for the good of the team or country. Throughout his adulthood, this lesson was buttressed by his conservative Lutheranism, which taught him that a man's first responsibility was as a family breadwinner, which meant to work hard and sacrifice himself, day in and day out, for the good of his family.

Indeed, as my mother cared for me and my two sisters, my father worked very hard during the school year as a high school teacher and a coach and on summer "tours" in the navy reserve. He prided himself that he had never let a little cold or flu or a sore back keep him from work. He'd been taught to "play through the pain," to keep his complaints to himself, never to show his own hurt, pain, or fears. When he started having trouble with his bowels, he ignored it and started to use more laxatives. When he spotted a bit of blood in his stool, he denied it, explained it away as perhaps a piece of tomato. He finally went to the doctor when he couldn't stand it any longer but by then it was too late. He died with nearly a year's worth of accumulated "sick leave" at the high school.

I've come to see my father's story as paradigmatic of the story of men in general. The promise of public status and masculine privilege comes with a price tag: Often, men pay with poor health, shorter lives, emotionally shallow relationships, and less time spent with loved ones. Indeed, the current gap between women's and men's life expectancy is about 7 years; men tend to consume tobacco and alcohol at higher rates than do women, resulting in higher rates of heart disease, cirrhosis of the liver, and lung cancer; men tend to be slower than women to ask for professional medical help; men tend to engage in violence and high-risk behavior at much higher rates than do women; and men are taught to downplay or ignore their own pain (Harrison, Chin, & Ficarratto, 1995; Sabo, 1994b; Sabo & Gordon, 1995; Stillion, 1995; Waldron, 1995). In short, conformity with narrow definitions of masculinity can be lethal for men. This, then, reflects a second theme that this book will develop.

Men tend to pay heavy costs—in the form of shallow relationships, poor health, and early death—for conformity with the narrow definitions of masculinity that promise to bring them status and privilege.

Differences and Inequalities Among Men

In the early 1980s, at one of the first National Conferences on Men and Masculinity, I sat with several hundred men and listened to a radical feminist male exhort all of us to "renounce masculinity" and "give up all of our male privileges" as we unite with women to work for a just and egalitarian world. Shortly after this moving speech, a black man stood up and angrily shouted, "When you ask me to give up my privileges as a man, you are asking me to give up something that white America has never allowed me in the first place! I've never been allowed to *be* a man in this racist society." After a smattering of applause and confused chatter, another man stood and said, "Yeah—I feel the same way as a gay man. My struggle is not to learn how to cry and hug other men. That's what you straight guys are all hung up on. I am oppressed in this homophobic society and need to empower myself to fight that oppression. I can't relate to your guilt-tripping us all into *giving up* our power. What power?"

This meeting illustrated one of the major issues faced by feminists, especially beginning in the 1980s: Women and men of color, gay men and lesbians, and differently abled people have all challenged the simplistic assumption that we can neatly discuss "women" and "men" as discrete categories within which members are assumed to share certain life experiences, life chances, and worldviews (Baca Zinn, Cannon, Higgenbotham, & Dill, 1986; Collins, 1990; Wittig, 1992). In fact, although it may be true that "men, as a group, enjoy institutional privileges at the expense of women, as a group," men share very unequally in the fruits of these privileges. Indeed, one can make a good case that the economic, political, and legal constraints facing poor African American, Latino, or Native American men, institutionally disenfranchised disabled men, illegal immigrant men, and some gay men more than overshadow whatever privileges these people might have as men in this society (Anderson, 1990; Gerschick & Miller, 1995; Hondagneu-Sotelo & Messner, 1994; Nonn, 1995; Staples, 1995a). And the "costs of masculinity," such as poor health and shorter life expectancy are paid out disproportionately by socially and economically marginalized men (Sabo, 1995; Staples, 1995a).

When we examine gender relations along with race and ethnicity, social class, sexuality, and age as crosscutting, interrelated systems of power and inequality, it becomes clear that studying men and women is far more complicated than it might first have seemed. In fact, as R. W. Connell (1987) has argued, it makes little sense to talk of a singular masculinity (or femininity, for that matter) as did much of the 1970s "sex role" literature. Instead, Connell observes that at any given historical moment there are various and competing masculinit*ies*. Hegemonic masculinity, the form of masculinity that is dominant, expresses (for the moment) a successful strategy for the domination of women, and it is also constructed in relation to various marginalized and subordinated masculinities (e.g., gay, black, and working-class masculinities). This is the third theme that will run through this book:

> *Men share very unequally in the fruits of patriarchy; hegemonic (white, middle- and upper-class, and heterosexual) masculinity is constructed in relation to femininities and to various (racial, sexual, and class) subordinated masculinities.*

These, then, are the three themes that underlie the examinations of men and masculinities in this book: Men, as a group, enjoy privileges due to the social construction of gender relations. Men tend to pay heavy costs for their adherence to narrow definitions of masculinity. Because there are such vast differences and inequalities among men, it's impossible even to talk honestly about men *as* a coherent group. If these three themes seem contradictory or paradoxical, it's because they are. But I am convinced that we can best approximate a clear understanding of contemporary gender relations if we try constantly to keep all three of these themes as central to our analysis as possible.

Men's Responses to
Historical Crises in the Gender Order

The social significance of Robert Bly's (1990) book did not lie in its groundbreaking nature; in fact, its publication came in the wake of a succession of scores of books about men since the mid-1970s (Carrigan, Connell, & Lee, 1987). The main significance of the book was that it was the first about men to gain prominence as a national best-seller. Indeed, the book sparked widespread discussion and debate and provided grist for journalists, cartoonists, and television shows such as *Murphy Brown* to lampoon "the sensitive man." And the book also had another important effect; for the first time, the notion of a "men's movement" was on the national agenda.

In the early 1990s, Bly's mythopoetic men's movement had, for all intents and purposes, become *the* men's movement in the popular discourse. But the mythopoetic movement is by no means the first or the only organized movement by men that has aimed to deal with gender issues or men's issues. In fact, some historians of masculinities argue that the past century has seen various crisis points in gender relations, to which men (or particular groups of men) have responded in various ways (Filene, 1975). Drawing from this historical research, sociologist Michael Kimmel (1987b, 1996) argues that men in the United States experienced a profound "crisis of masculinity" around the turn of the 20th century. In this era, white, middle-class men, especially, perceived a threat to the meaning of hegemonic masculinity and to their positions of power relative to women and to lower-class men, due to a combination of changes brought on by modernization of social life and by the rise of organized feminist movements. Kimmel (1987a) argues that men's organized responses to the crisis of masculinity varied and can be categorized as "masculinist," "antifeminist," or "profeminist."

Modernization was characterized by the closing of the frontier, industrialization, urbanization, the rise of modern bureaucracies (with the resultant decline of the significance of physical strength in most middle-class occupations), and the fact that modern urban boys were increasingly separated from their fathers and placed in the care of mothers (in homes) or female schoolteachers. The resultant changes in work and family life brought on by modernization led to "fears of social feminization," especially among middle-class men. Some men responded to these fears with the creation of homosocial spheres of life such as the Boy Scouts of America (Hantover, 1978), organized sports (Messner, 1992), fraternal orders and lodges (Clawson, 1989), and college fraternities (Lefkowitz-Horowitz, 1987). Filene (1975) observes that the first crisis of masculinity came to a temporary end with the outset of World War I, when many young males enthusiastically saw war as the ultimate homosocial institution within which to prove their manhood. In short, masculinist responses to men's fears of social feminization resulted in men's creation of (or in the case of the military, attraction to existing) homosocial institutions in which adult men, separated from women, could engage in "masculine" activities, often centered around the development and celebration of physical strength, competition, and violence. Some of them (Boy Scouts, sports) were institutions in which fathers hoped to initiate their sons into manhood through physical activities that were viewed as masculine returns to "nature" that they hoped would counterbalance the "feminizing" effect of modern urban social life.

The second factor that Kimmel (1987a) points to as stimulating the turn-of-the-century crisis of masculinity was the rise of organized women's movements. Whereas masculinist creations of homosocial institutions can be seen more as men's organized responses to modernization, antifeminist and profeminist responses are more direct responses to women's organized movements for equality and empowerment. Antifeminist organizations, such as groups that actively opposed women's suffrage, can be viewed as direct attempts to maintain patriarchal control of the state. By contrast, profeminist men, such as those who actively supported the growth of women's colleges and men who marched in demonstrations in support of women's suffrage in the early years of the 20th century, saw the emancipation of women as linked to a larger effort to expand democracy and equality to all people (Kimmel & Mosmiller, 1992).

In our current era, beginning especially in the 1960s, a similar configuration of changes in work and family relations, along with the resurgence of feminism, has brought about a renewed crisis of masculinity, to which men are again responding in a variety of ways (Kimmel, 1996). Although not disagreeing with Kimmel's analysis of the impact of modernization and feminism on men's lives, R. W. Connell (1995) argues that the notion of a "crisis of masculinity" is problematic:

> As a theoretical term, "crisis" presupposes a coherent system of some kind, which is destroyed or restored by the outcome of the crisis. Masculinity . . . is not a system in that sense. It is, rather, a configuration of practice *within* a system of gender relations. We cannot logically speak of the crisis of a configuration; rather we might speak of its disruption or its transformation. We can, however, logically speak of the crisis of the gender order as a whole, and of its tendencies toward crisis. (p. 84)

Connell (1995) identifies three broad areas in which the current gender order exhibits "crisis tendencies." First, "*Power relations* show the most visible evidence of crisis tendencies: a historic collapse of the legitimacy of patriarchal power and a global movement for the emancipation of women." Though "collapse" surely overstates the extent to which patriarchal relations have transformed, it is undeniably˙ true that feminist movements throughout the world have challenged and contested men's institutional power and the ideas that support this power. Second, Connell argues that "*Production relations* have also been the site of massive institutional changes. Most notable are the vast postwar growth in married women's employment in rich countries, and the even vaster incorporation of women's labour into the money economy in poor countries." In the U.S. context, I would also add the notable decline—especially during the past two decades of deindustialization—in the number of stable unionized, family-wage-paying jobs for blue-collar men. This decline has been accompanied by an increase in low-paying, service sector jobs (occupied disproportionately by women and recent immigrants) and a rise in the level of "normal" structural unemployment. Third, Connell asserts that "*Relations of cathexis* have visibly changed with the stabilization of lesbian and gay sexuality as a public alternative within the heterosexual order" (pp. 84-85). In other words, the very existence of gay and lesbian communities, public debates about gays in the military and gay and lesbian marriages tends to destabilize the previously taken-for-granted assumptions about the relationship between sexual orientation and cultural notions about gender, families, and masculine institutions such as the military.

Recent Men's Movements: Mapping the Terrain

In this book, I begin with Connell's view of masculinities as multiple configurations of gender practice, responding to current crises in power relations with women, work and the economy, and sexuality. But my focus is somewhat different from Connell's. Connell uses the life history method to demonstrate how individual men who are situated differently in relation to crisis tendencies in the gender order—for instance, young men in declining blue-collar industrial occupations—have responded by constructing varied identities and practices of gender and sexuality. I am more concerned here with men's *organized responses* to these crisis tendencies. In what follows, I will outline what I see to be eight major tendencies in groups that, beginning in the early 1970s and stretching through the present, have attempted to engage in a conscious politics of masculinities: men's liberationists, men's rights advocates, radical feminist men, socialist feminist men, men of color, gay male liberationists, Promise Keepers, and the mythopoetic men's movement.

To grapple with this complex range of movements, I will introduce and use a conceptual model that I call the "terrain of the politics of masculinities." I use this model as a tool for comparing and critically evaluating the varying political discourses and actions in the politics of masculinities. As you can see in Figure 1.1, the terrain of the politics of masculinities appears as a geographical triad.

Earlier, I introduced the three themes that represent the three points of this conceptual triad when I argued that a critical sociological under-

FIGURE 1.1

The Terrain of the Politics of Masculinities

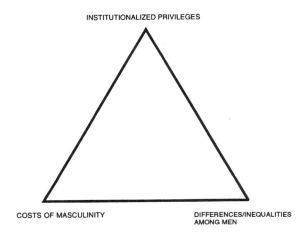

INSTITUTIONALIZED PRIVILEGES

COSTS OF MASCULINITY   DIFFERENCES/INEQUALITIES
                                        AMONG MEN

standing of masculinities must simultaneously take into account three factors: (a) men's institutionalized privileges, (b) the costs attached to adherence to narrow conceptions of masculinity, and (c) differences and inequalities among men. In subsequent chapters, I will demonstrate that each of the eight contemporary men's movements occupies a particular location within this terrain of the politics of masculinities and that this location is determined by which of these three factors—privileges, costs, differences—are emphasized and foregrounded, or alternatively rendered to the background or even ignored. Furthermore, I will argue that each movement's points of emphasis—and its blind spots—result in critically important political possibilities, limits, and/or dangers. One of the key issues here concerns the ways in which these groups understand and organize around *men's interests*—or around particular groups of men's interests. Put very simply, groups that are positioned roughly in the lower half of the triad tend to feel that it is in the interests of men (or particular groups of men) to organize to gain more power and control over their lives. The call for "male empowerment" tends to be very attractive to many men who do not feel particularly powerful or privileged. Conversely, groups that are positioned in the upper half of the triad are organized largely around the goal of *undermining* men's institutional power and privileges over women. As we shall see, this profeminist belief—that it is in men's interest as human beings to organize in order to undermine their own narrowly defined economic, political, and interpersonal power over women—has not proved to have a very wide appeal to many men. The overarching purpose of this book, then, is to introduce a conceptual model through which we might begin to make sense of the otherwise confusing array of organized attempts by men to grapple with the meaning of manhood. In particular, my aim is to locate various discourses and practices of contemporary "politics of masculinities" within the larger terrain of gender politics. But why focus on politics? To be sure, one could examine and evaluate these organized expressions of masculinities in a number of ways. For instance, one could examine men's movements and organizations in terms of their therapeutic or spiritual impact on participants. Or one could focus on the interpersonal level and ask whether participation in these various organizations has an impact on the types and quality of intimate relationships, friendships, and work relationships that men have with other men, children, or women. My decision to examine these men's movements mostly in terms of their actual or potential *political* impact is grounded in my commitment to the goal of social justice. According to Connell (1995), the pursuit of social justice

> in most cases means the pursuit of equality. . . . Pursuing social justice in power relations means contesting men's predominance in the state, professions, and management, and ending men's violence against women. . . . Pursuing social justice in the gender division of labour means ending the patriarchal dividend in the money economy, sharing the burden of domestic work, and equalizing access to education and training (still massively unequal on a world scale). Pursuing social justice in the structure of cathexis means ending the stigma of sexual difference and the imposition of compulsory heterosexuality, and reconstructing heterosexuality on the basis of reciprocity, not hierarchy. . . . Social justice in gender relations, understood in this way, is a generalizable interest but not a demand for uniformity. (pp. 229-230)

I would add to Connell's agenda the provision that the pursuit of social justice in gender and sexual relations necessarily connects with the pursuit of social justice in economic, racial, and ethnic relations. In short, I believe that groups that have organized their discourse and practices around "men's issues" or "men and masculinity" have done so as a response to current shifts and crisis tendencies in the relations of power between and among women and men. The practices of such groups will inevitably have an impact on this political terrain—whether the dominant discourse of the group is overtly "political" or not. Thus, the fundamental question about such groups—indeed, I would argue, the fundamental question that should underlie any sociological examination of contemporary masculinities—is to what extent their actual or potential political impact will impede or advance movements for social justice (Messner, 1990).

To conclude this chapter, I would like to anticipate some questions that readers might raise about the utility of my terrain of the politics of masculinities model in helping us make sense of a very complex moment in the history of gender relations. First, any such analysis of political tendencies runs the risk of creating conceptual categories that ignore overlap between groups and fragmentation and difference within groups. For instance, the fact that my schema names and locates political tendencies that I am calling "men of color," "gay male liberationists," and "radical feminist men" may suggest that these are entirely separate and discrete categories. But where, then, do gay men of color fit? And where do radical feminist gay men of color fit? In fact, I hope to argue that rather than reifying these categories, the conceptual schema that I am introducing here can serve as a tool to highlight the problems inherent in a politics of identity that foregrounds *either* race and ethnicity *or* sexual orientation *or* gender. In short, rather than looking for (or working to construct) bridges, the politics of identity too often serves to (falsely) highlight shared experiences within groups that, in turn, serve to obliterate difference and inequalities within the group as well as similarities with other groups. My intention, then, is to introduce and use these eight tendencies as ideal types, as constructs that summarize, albeit in a simplified way, the political discourse of real groups of people who are currently engaged in the politics of masculinities. My aim is to develop this schema as a conceptual tool that may be useful in identifying bridges and intersections where some of these groups might meet, with the goal of transcending single-issue politics in favor of broad progressive coalition building.

Organization of the Book

I will divide my examination of eight political tendencies in the contemporary politics of U.S. masculinities into four major groups. In Chapter 2, I will focus on what I call "essentialist retreats" from feminism: the mythopoetic men's movement and the fundamentalist Christian Promise Keepers. In Chapter 3, I will discuss the limits of liberal responses to contemporary crises in the gender order by tracking how a major part of the early 1970s men's liberation movement eventually devolved into an antifeminist men's rights movement. Chapter 4 will focus on men's "radical engagements" with feminism: radical feminism and socialist feminism. Chapter 5 will analyze "men's identity politics" that include the racialized masculinity politics of men of color and gay male liberationism. In Chapter 6, I will explore some actual or potential points of intersection between some of these groups. Here, I will discuss to what extent an organized, profeminist men's movement can serve as a locus for activity by men aimed at contributing to the development of social justice. Finally, I will suggest that recent perspectives that have been introduced by feminist women of color offer the most promising position today from which to establish a progressive politics of masculinities.

CHAPTER 2

Essentialist Retreats

The Mythopoetic Men's Movement and the Christian Promise Keepers

> There's a general assumption now that every man in a position of power is or soon will be corrupt and oppressive. Yet the Greeks understood and praised a positive male energy that has accepted authority. They called it Zeus energy, which encompasses intelligence, robust health, compassionate decisiveness, good will, generous leadership. Zeus energy is male authority accepted for the sake of the community.
>
> —*Robert Bly (1990, p. 61)*

> Christian men all over our nation and around the world are suffering because they feel they are on a losing streak and they can't break the pattern. . . . God's eyes are moving to and fro for men with a full passion for the gospel message. The Lord is calling men from across our nation to lead a new uprising of men filled with God's Spirit. Now is the time for that uprising.
>
> —*Bill McCartney (1992, p. 13)*

Because feminism has had such a profound effect on U.S. society over the past three decades, it is virtually impossible for men to entirely avoid confronting "gender issues" in daily life, whether in personal relations, schools, workplaces, or the media. But some men clearly have made collective attempts to disengage themselves from feminism. The irony is that these organized attempts to grapple with the meanings of masculinity by retreating from women would not exist if feminism had not raised "the man question" in the first place. The two groups I will focus on in this chapter—the mythopoetic men's movement and the Christian Promise Keepers—are movements of men that have grown with astonishing rapidity in recent years. Although these movements differ in some important ways, they are strikingly similar in other ways. Leaders of both share an aversion to what they see as a recent "feminization" of men. The mythopoetic movement, though, is more apt to blame modernization for this feminization of men, whereas Promise Keepers is more apt to blame feminism, gay liberation, sexual liberation, and the "breakdown of the family" for men's problems. Both groups see a need for men to retreat from women to create spiritually based homosocial rituals through which they can collectively recapture a lost or strayed "true manhood." And these movements are asserting men's responsibility to retake their natural positions of leadership in their communities.

The Mythopoetic
Men's Movement

The mythopoetic men's movement began quietly in the 1980s with a few men attending lectures and weekend retreats. By 1990, thousands of men—most of them white, middle-aged, heterosexual, and of the professional class—had attended mythopoetic events, and Robert Bly's book, *Iron John*, was a national best-seller. Through the use of old fairy tales and poetry, Bly and other mythopoetic leaders, such as Michael Meade and James Hillman, attempted to guide men on spiritual journeys aimed at rediscovering and reclaiming "the deep masculine" parts of themselves that they believed had been lost. In a nutshell, Bly argues that tribal societies had masculinity rituals, through which adult men initiated boys into a deeply essential (natural) manhood. Furthermore, urban industrial society, by severing the ritual ties between the generations of men and replacing them with alienating, competitive, and bureaucratic bonds, obliterated masculinity rituals, thus cutting men off from each other and ultimately from their own deep masculine natures. In place of these healthy masculinity rituals, as Bly's (1990) words suggest, modern men revert either to destructive hypermasculinity or to a "femininity" that softens and deadens their masculine, life-affirming potential:

> We have to accept the possibility that the true radiant energy in the male does not hide in, reside in, or wait for us in the feminine realm, nor in the macho/John Wayne realm, but in the magnetic field of the deep masculine. It is protected by the *instinctive* one who's underwater and who has been there we don't know how long. (p. 8)

Bly's curious interpretations of mythology, his highly selective use of history, psychology, and anthropology, and his essentialist ("instinctive") assumptions about masculinity, which run counter to the past 30 years of social scientific research on the social construction of gender, have been soundly criticized as shoddy scholarship (e.g., Connell, 1992; Kimmel, 1992; Kimmel & Kaufman, 1994). But more important than a critique of Bly's ideas is a sociological interpretation of why the mythopoetic men's movement has attracted so many predominantly white, college-educated, middle-class, middle-aged men in the United States over the past decade. I suspect that Bly's movement attracts these men *not* because it represents any sort of radical break from "traditional masculinity" but precisely because it is so congruent with shifts that are already taking place within current constructions of hegemonic masculinity.

First, mythopoetic discourse appears congruent with the contemporary resurgence of belief in essential differences between women and men. Michael Schwalbe (1996), who has conducted the only systematic sociological study of mythopoetic men, has noted that the Jungian basis of the mythopoetic belief system has laid the groundwork for a complex and contradictory "loose essentialism." On the one hand, mythopoetic men tend to treat "gender, masculinity, and the category 'men' as if they were primitive constituent elements of the universe" rather than social constructions (p. 66). This belief in essential natures of women and men appealed to mythopoetic men because

> it provided an ideological defense against feminist criticisms of men. Such a defense was necessary precisely because the men saw it as natural. The men were aware of generic feminist criticisms of men as brutish, insensitive, power hungry, and so on. However, the men did not see these criticisms as aimed at social arrangements that produced a lot of genuinely bad men. Rather, they interpreted these . . . as criticisms of the essential nature of men. Feminist criticism of men was thus experienced as indicting the morality of all men. A defense had to respond in kind; it had to somehow redeem the category. (p. 64)

This essentialist redemption of the category "men" in effect allows mythopoetic men to assert, "This is what I am as a man—take it or leave it. I won't feel guilty about it. I won't apologize for my gender" (Schwalbe, 1996, p. 65). On the other hand, Schwalbe argues, the "loose essentialism" that mythopoetic men subscribe to allows for agency and flexibility in individual men's constructions of their own masculinity. In short, mythopoetic men's work offers a collective ritual structure within which individual men can explore, discover, and reconstruct their inner selves. As Schwalbe (1996) summed it up,

The reason *loose* essentialism was so appealing is that it left room for change. A stricter form of essentialism would have implied that a man's way of being was immutable. . . . Loose essentialism, however, allowed the mythopoetic men to have it both ways. They got the moral license for possessing the feminine and masculine traits they already had, and they got the theoretical possibility of changing what they wanted to change. (p. 65)

There do appear to be several things that mythopoetic men would like to change. Many of the men who attend mythopoetic gatherings are acutely aware of some of the problems, limits, and costs that are attached to narrow conceptions of masculinity. A major preoccupation of men at mythopoetic gatherings is the poverty of men's relationships with fathers and with other men in workplaces. These concerns are based on real and often painful experiences. Indeed, industrial capitalism undermined much of the structural basis of middle-class men's emotional bonds with each other, as wage labor, market competition, and instrumental rationality largely supplanted primogeniture, craft brotherhood, and intergenerational mentorship (Clawson, 1989; Tolson, 1977). Mythopoetic "male initiation" rituals are intended to heal and reconstruct these masculine bonds, and they are thus probably experienced as largely irrelevant to men's relationships with women (Kimmel & Kaufman, 1994).

But in focusing on how myth and ritual can reconnect men with each other, and ultimately with their own deep masculine essences as a means of dealing with men's pain, mythopoetic discourse and practice manage to sidestep the central point of the feminist critique—that men, as a group, benefit from a structure of power that oppresses women, as a group. The "loose essentialism" that underlies mythopoetic thought does allow these men to "have it both ways," as Schwalbe (1996) has pointed out. They can ignore—or even become defensive about—feminist criticisms of men's institutional power and privileges. At the same time, they can construct practices that confront their own major preoccupation with the "costs of masculinity" or, in mythopoetic terms, with "men's wounds." To reflect this primary focus on the costs of masculinity, I locate the mythopoetic men's movement toward the lower left corner of the terrain of the politics of masculinities (see Figure 2.1).

In ignoring the social structure of power, Bly and other mythopoetic leaders conveyed a false symmetry between the feminist women's movement and the mythopoetic men's movement. Bly (1990) assumes a natural dichotomization of "male values" and "female values" and

FIGURE 2.1

The Terrain of the Politics of Masculinities: The Mythopoetic Men's Movement and Promise Keepers

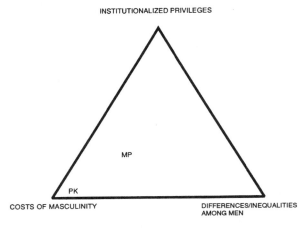

INSTITUTIONALIZED PRIVILEGES

MP

PK

COSTS OF MASCULINITY   DIFFERENCES/INEQUALITIES
                                        AMONG MEN

PK = Promise Keepers
MP = Mythopoetic Men's Movement

states that feminism has been good for women, in allowing them to reassert "the feminine voice" that had been suppressed. But Bly states (and he carefully avoids directly blaming feminism for this), "the masculine voice" has now been muted—men have become "passive . . . tamed . . . domesticated." Men thus need a movement to reconnect with the "Zeus energy" that they have lost. And "Zeus energy is male authority accepted for the good of the community" (p. 61).

At least on its surface, this mythopoetic discourse appears to be part of a contemporary antifeminist backlash (Faludi, 1991). But Michael Schwalbe (1995a, 1996) observes that most mythopoetic men are not overtly concerned with creating a backlash against feminist women—in fact, they are not consciously attempting to articulate a rational political vision or practice at all. They believe that industrial society has trapped men into straitjackets of rationality, thus blunting the powerful emotional communion and collective spiritual transcendence that they believe men in tribal societies typically enjoyed. Schwalbe notes that there is a "widening recognition" in society today that social problems are not technical ones that can be solved by science or rationalism. "Into this breach of faith have stepped fundamentalist religion and various New Age philosophies. Jungian psychology [the major basis of mythopoetic thought] has also found a niche in the gap between science and religion. . . . Jungian psychology sends us back to the unconscious" (Schwalbe, 1996, p. 67). Thus, mythopoetic discourse is at its core antimodernist and antirationalist, and the aims of mythopoetic practice are primarily therapeutic and spiritual. Schwalbe (1995a) describes mythopoetic men as

> selectively apolitical. They did not want to see that it was other *men* who were responsible for many of the social problems they witnessed and were sometimes affected by. To do so, and to talk about it, would have shattered the illusion of brotherhood among the men. . . . The mythopoetic men believed that engaging in political or sociological analysis would have led them away from their goals of self-acceptance, self-knowledge, emotional authenticity, and *communitas*. . . . They wanted untroubled brotherhood in which their feelings were validated by other men, and in which their identities as men could be infused with new value. (p. 517)

The implications of this anti-intellectual and apolitical core of mythopoetic discourse were brought home to me when I attended a mythopoetic event a few years ago. In a speech to these men, I presented what I hoped was a carefully reasoned argument, grounded in social scientific research; in short, when we look at nonindustrial societies, we see that the more rape-prone societies tend to be those that have high levels of male-dominated sex segregation in public spaces and those that celebrate war (Sanday, 1981). Thus, I concluded, it seemed dangerous that the mythopoetic men were celebrating the image of "the male warrior," within the context of their expressed need to create homosocial rituals that emphasized and reinforced men's separation from women. To this, the mythopoetic men responded that the form of my analysis and critique was an example of "traditional masculine" discourse. They had no interest in engaging in "rational, sociological analysis" of what they were doing. In fact, this kind of rational analytical thought ran counter to the largely spiritual and emotional men's work that they were engaged in. I (and the rest of the guests) were invited from this point on to share only thoughts that came "from the heart, not from the head."

This anti-intellectual stance, in effect, insulated the group from dealing with criticisms or troubling questions about how their "men's work" might fit in with concrete social relations, power, and inequality. But despite its apolitical intent, the political implications of mythopoetic discourse and practice can still be critically analyzed. First and foremost, the mythopoetic notion that men need to be empowered *as men* echoes the views of some of the early men's liberation activists (to be discussed in Chapter 3), who saw men and women as "equally oppressed" by sexism. But the view that "everyone is oppressed by sexism" strips the concept of "oppression" of its political meaning and obscures the social relations of domination and subordination. *Oppression* is a concept that describes a relationship between social groups; for one group to be oppressed, there must be an oppressor group (Freire, 1970). This is not to imply that an oppressive relationship between groups is absolute or static. To the contrary, oppression is characterized by a constant and complex state of play. Oppressed groups actively participate in their own domination and actively resist that domination. The state of play of the contemporary gender order is characterized by men's individual and collective oppression of women (Connell, 1987). Men continue to benefit from this oppression of women but, importantly, in the past 30 years, women's compliance with masculine hegemony has been counterbalanced by active feminist resistance.

Men do tend to pay a price for their power. They are often emotionally limited and commonly suffer poor health and a shorter life expectancy than women. These problems, however, are best viewed not as gender oppression but as the "costs of being on top" (Kann, 1986)—or at least of *trying* to be on top. This is well illustrated by recent shifts in masculine styles that we see among privileged men. These shifts indicate that these men would like to stop paying these costs but not that they desire to cease being "on top." In recent years, it has become commonplace to see powerful and successful men weeping in public: Ronald Reagan shedding a tear at the funeral of slain U.S. soldiers, basketball player Michael Jordan openly crying after winning the NBA championship. In this shifting context, I would argue that the easy manner in which the media lauded U.S. General Schwartzkopf as a "new man" for shedding a public tear for the U.S. casualties in the Persian Gulf is indicative of the importance placed on *styles of masculine gender display* rather than the institutional *position of power* that men such as Schwartzkopf still enjoy.

What this emphasis on the significance of public displays of crying indicates, in part, is a naive belief that if boys and men can learn to "express their feelings," they will no longer feel a need to dominate others. This assumption is based partly on the fact that much of the earlier research on men and masculinity was conducted by psychologists who tended to focus on the "tragedy" of "male inexpressivity" but ignored the social structures of power within which male personalities are constructed (e.g., Balswick & Peek, 1971). In a highly influential critique of the psychological literature on male inexpressivity, Jack Sattel (1976) argued,

> A boy must become inexpressive not simply because our culture expects little boys to be inexpressive but because our culture expects little boys to grow up to become decision-makers and wielders of power. . . . To effectively wield power, one must be able both to convince others of the rightness of the decisions one makes and to guard against one's own emotional involvement in the consequences of that decision; that is, one has to show that decisions are reached rationally and efficiently. One must also be able to close one's eyes to the potential pain one's decisions have for others and one's self. (pp. 470-471)

Sattel's perspective would imply that, although "male inexpressivity" is socially constructed, mere therapeutic interventions to get individual men to "open up" will have a limited appeal unless we also change the structural positions of power that men have been expected to hold. But for men of the professional classes, these positions—and thus the types of personalities that it takes to operate within these positions—may have been shifting in recent decades. Clearly, the kind of masculine personality that was ascendant (hegemonic) during the rise of entrepreneurial capitalism was extremely instrumental, stoic, and emotionally inexpressive (Winter & Robert, 1980). But there is growing evidence (e.g., Schwartzkopf) that today there is no longer a neat link between class-privileged men's emotional inexpressivity and their willingness and ability to dominate others (Connell, 1991). Perhaps a situationally appropriate public display of sensitivity such as crying, rather than signaling weakness, has become a legitimizing sign of the "new man's" class status (Hondagneu-Sotelo & Messner, 1994; Messner, 1993a).

Thus, relatively privileged men may be attracted to the mythopoetic men's movement because, on the one hand, it acknowledges and validates their painful "wounds," while guiding them to connect with other men in ways that are nurturing and mutually empowering. On the other hand, and unlike feminism, it does not confront men with the reality of how their own privileges are based on the continued subordination of women and other men. In short, the mythopoetic men's movement may be seen as facilitating the reconstruction of a new form of hegemonic

masculinity—a masculinity that is less self-destructive, that has reval-
ued and reconstructed men's emotional bonds with each other, and that
has learned to feel good about its own "Zeus power."

Promise Keepers

In 1995, 600,000 Christian men, led by Bill McCartney, packed several football stadiums throughout the United States to listen to sermons,
sing, and pray about their roles as men. The rapid growth of McCartney's Christian men's organization, Promise Keepers, has been dramatic. Launched with its first meeting in 1990 with only 72 men in
attendance, the organization's yearly meeting swelled to 4,200 in 1991,
22,000 in 1992, and 50,000 in 1993. In 1994, 278,600 men attended
Promise Keepers rallies in seven cities, and in 1995, over 600,000 men
reportedly attended Promise Keepers meetings in 13 cities in the United
States. The Promise Keepers organization raises about 3 million dollars
per event, and the money is spent on organizing future rallies and on
developing a nationwide network of men. Their phenomenal growth
rate led organizers to plan a mass rally in 1996, preceding the U.S.
presidential elections, where they hoped "that 1 million men will de-
scend on Washington to kneel in prayer and ask God for forgiveness as
men—and to restore America" (Sahagun, 1995, p. A1). But Promise
Keepers decided to put off its own rally in Washington D.C. until
perhaps 1997 after hearing of the plan by African Americans for their
own 1996 Million Man March on the Capitol (to be discussed in Chapter 5).

Promise Keepers may seem to have suddenly appeared from virtually nowhere, but in fact, there is a historical ebb and flow of overt
masculinity politics within fundamentalist Christianity in the United
States. And the "flow" tends to follow in the wake of feminist challenges
to taken-for-granted assumptions about men's positions of authority in
families and in communities. Shortly after the turn of the 20th century,
during what is now commonly known as the "first wave of feminism,"
a popular wave of "Muscular Christianity" swept the United States. The
most famous Muscular Christian leader was an evangelist named Billy
Sunday. Like Promise Keepers' most visible leader Bill McCartney a
century later, Sunday entered his ministry after a successful career in
sports (he had played professional baseball), and according to one
journalist of the time, he "brought bleacher-crazy, frenzied aggression
to religion" (as cited in Kimmel, 1996, p. 179). Muscular Christianity

was part of a larger turn-of-the-century masculine response to a crisis of masculinity brought on by feminism, modernization, and widespread fears that boys and men were becoming "feminized." According to Kimmel (1996),

> The goal of the Muscular Christians was to reviralize the image of Jesus and thus remasculinize the Church. Jesus was "no dough-faced, lickspittle proposition," proclaimed evangelist Billy Sunday, but "the greatest scrapper who ever lived." Look to Jesus, counseled Luther Gulick of the YMCA, for an example of "magnificent manliness." Books such as *The Harvest Within* (1909), *Building the Young Man* (1912), *The Call of the Carpenter* (1913), *The Manhood of the Master* (1913), *The Manliness of Christ* (1900), *The Manly Christ* (1904), and *The Masculine Power of Christ* (1912) portrayed Jesus as a brawny carpenter, whose manly resolve challenged the idolators, kicked the money changers out of the temple, and confronted the most powerful imperium ever assembled. He was no "Prince of peace at any price." (p. 177)

Muscular Christian organizations, such as the Men and Religion Forward Movement of 1911-1912, "swept the country like a spiritual storm," increasing the number of men coming to church by up to 800% in some communities (Kimmel, 1996, p. 181). More recently, in the wake of the second wave of feminism, a similarly virile version of fundamentalist Christianity began to emerge in the United States. Its first stirrings appeared in the 1970s as a right-wing Christian movement flexing its muscles in opposition to feminism, gay and lesbian liberation, and sexual liberation (e.g., Falwell, 1981; Schlafly, 1981). By the early to mid-1980s, an overt politics of masculinity had begun to coalesce within this conservative Christian coalition, especially in the teachings of Edwin Louis Cole. In his early 1980s workshops, television appearances, and cassette tapes, Cole began to articulate a late 20th-century version of Muscular Christianity. For instance, in his 1982 book, *Maximized Manhood*, Cole assures men that "women just want [men] to be the leaders in the home in every way" (p. 77). Echoing the views of the Muscular Christians, Cole passionately argues that the model for masculine toughness and leadership is Jesus himself:

> Some "sissified" paintings of Jesus come nowhere near showing the real character of Him who was both Son of Man and Son of God. Jesus was a fearless leader, defeating Satan, casting out demons, commanding nature, rebuking hypocrites. . . . God wants to reproduce this manhood

in all men. . . . Since to be like Jesus—Christlike—requires a certain ruthlessness, manhood does also. (p. 63)

By the early 1990s, this call for a remasculinized image of Jesus, and its concomitant call for men to retake leadership roles in families, had become the central message of Promise Keepers. For example, Promise Keepers leader Dr. Tony Evans (1994) stated,

> I am convinced that the primary cause of this national crisis is the feminization of the American male. When I say *feminization,* I am not talking about sexual preference. I'm trying to describe a misunderstanding of manhood that has produced a nation of "sissified" men who abdicate their role as spiritually pure leaders, thus forcing women to fill the vacuum. (p. 73)

This fear of male feminization and call for a remasculinization of men has clearly caught on among certain groups of Christian men. Sociologist Jay Coakley (1993), who attended the 1992 meeting of Promise Keepers in Colorado, observed that most of the men appeared to be "between 35 and 50 years old . . . and at least 98% of them were white, and most were middle or upper middle class" (p. 1). The discourse, Coakley observed, was also exclusively heterosexual. Observers of 1995 rallies agree that the organization remains a predominantly white, male, middle-class Protestant and heterosexual affair (Sahagun, 1995; Stoltenberg, 1995). But in 1996, Promise Keepers organized its conferences around the theme of "Break Down the Walls," with the stated intention of directly confronting racial barriers between men. The 1996 rallies all included prominent religious leaders from African American, Latino, Native American, and Asian American communities. And Promise Keepers' official magazine, *New Man,* focused many of its articles and photo spreads on the lives of Latino and Asian immigrant men and African American men. Despite this impressive aim to "break down" racial "walls" between men, Promise Keepers' demographic composition as still a mostly white organization (Leibowitz, 1996) and its stated aim to help men "reclaim the spiritual leadership in their families and communities" echo the white, middle-aged heterosexual mythopoetic movement's aim to reassert men's "Zeus power." But there are two significant differences between the mythopoetics and the Promise Keepers. The first is grounded in different ways that the two movements assert an essentialist view of masculinity; the second relates to their different views of what constitutes a desirable family structure.

Biblical Essentialism Reasserted

Whereas the mythopoetics' "loose" gender essentialism contains a belief in individual agency and flexibility in the shaping of gender, Promise Keepers relies entirely on a fundamentalist biblical interpretation of essentially fixed and categorically different natures of women and men. This categorical essentialism underlies Promise Keepers' rejection of feminist critiques of men's institutional power, and it encourages a blurring or ignoring of differences among men. Promise Keepers is, however, aware of and concerned with a number of problems that contemporary men share; thus, I locate it in the extreme "costs of masculinity" corner of the terrain of the politics of masculinities (see Figure 2.1). Promise Keepers argues that men's problems today result largely from *departures* from men's natural roles.

As a movement, Promise Keepers is on a leading edge of an antifeminist reassertion of essentialist views of male and female differences, a reassertion that expresses itself in religion, popular culture, and mainstream political life. For instance, in early 1995, Speaker of the U.S. House of Representatives Newt Gingrich explained why he thought that military women are not suited for combat duty: "If combat means living in a ditch," the Republican Congressman asserted, "females have a biological problem staying in a ditch for 30 days because they get infections. . . . Males are biologically driven to go out and hunt giraffes." Though many people were likely puzzled by the shortage of giraffes in their neighborhoods, Gingrich's statement reflected a widely held view that women and men are suited for different activities due to natural, inborn differences between the sexes.

This biological essentialism—the belief that women and men are essentially and categorically different—is grounded historically in conservative readings of Judeo-Christian texts, in Victorianism, in degenerate Freudianism, and in 19th- and early 20th-century medical science (Connell, 1995). A major implication of this kind of essentialism, as Gingrich's words suggest, is the assumption that there are natural, biological reasons for women and men to occupy different *social* positions, and not just in the military. The belief that women are biologically best suited for the care and nurturance of children but that men's tendency toward rationality and aggressive competition best suits them to be captains of industry or workers in the paid labor force has provided the foundation for the development of a gendered public-domestic split (that, until recent years, was most pronounced among the white, middle and upper classes). Essentialism also provided the justification (mostly in the past) for the belief that women should not be allowed to vote or hold political office and for the passing of protective legislation that barred women from doing certain jobs, for fear that these jobs would endanger their health (and especially their childbearing abilities).

By the beginning of the 1970s, a body of social scientific research had begun to emerge that demonstrated that nearly all of the things that we assumed were natural differences between women and men were in fact socially constructed. This kind of research led social scientists to insist on the use of two distinct concepts: *sex* and *gender*. Sex, social scientists argued, is a biological category that describes whether a person is male or female. Gender was proposed as a social category that describes the masculine or feminine traits that are socially assigned to biological males and females. Many of the differences that we considered to be "natural sex differences," this research revealed, were actually socially constructed gender differences. As Maccoby and Jacklin (1975) concluded from their survey of the sex difference research, though we assume women and men to be categorically different, in actuality, the research reveals that, despite some average differences, there is more overlap than difference between women's and men's physical traits, emotional states, and attitudes. This analytic distinction between biological sex and cultural gender provided a challenge to social inequalities that rest on essentialist thought.

But still, isn't it true that women's and men's bodies are fundamentally different? And doesn't it make sense that these differences, grounded in our biology, should have implications for the ways in which we organize and live our lives? For instance, it is common knowledge that because men have the hormone testosterone, they are naturally more physically powerful, aggressive, and violent than women. According to advocates of this view, patriarchy is "inevitable," and feminism is an affront to nature (Gilder, 1973; Goldberg, 1974). These beliefs can be summarized as a "common sense" causal proposition about the behavioral and social implications of supposed biological differences between men and women:

men have testosterone → men are more aggressive → men dominate women

First, this proposition begins with a *categorical* premise: "Men have testosterone." This premise is correct, except to the extent that it implies that women do *not* have testosterone. In fact, the common practice of calling testosterone a "male hormone" and estrogen a "female hormone" tends to mask the fact that women and men have *both*. On average, men do have about 10 times the amount of testosterone that women have. But the range of testosterone levels among men varies greatly, and some women actually have higher levels than do some men (Fausto-Sterling, 1985; Kemper, 1990).

Second, the above proposition implies that the existence of testosterone in males *causes* them to be naturally more physically powerful, aggressive, and violent than women. In fact, taken as a whole, the numerous studies that have aimed to establish a clear correlation between testosterone and aggression levels have been inconclusive (Fausto-Sterling, 1985; Pleck, 1982). Theodore Kemper (1990), in his fascinating book *Social Structure and Testosterone,* has argued that if there is a relationship between testosterone levels and aggression, it is clearly not a one-way causal relationship, as the above proposition implies. Kemper notes several studies that measured the links between men's changing testosterone levels and their experiences within specific social settings. These studies with tennis players, medical students, wrestlers, nautical competitors, officer candidates, and parachutists all came to remarkably similar conclusions. Put simply, "winners" experienced dramatic surges in testosterone levels; testosterone levels of the "losers" stayed the same or dropped. The key factors leading to men's testosterone surges are the experiences of *dominance*, which "refers to elevated social rank that is achieved by overcoming others in a competitive confrontation," and/or *eminence*, where "elevated social rank is earned through socially valued and approved accomplishment" (pp. 27-28). Significantly, these studies indicated that a man's "before" testosterone level could not be used to predict whether he would be a "winner" or a "loser." Instead, it was the *experience* of rising status due to one's successful efforts in a competitive endeavor that led to rising testosterone levels. Studies also suggest that the experience of dominance and eminence also leads to elevations in *women's* testosterone levels, thus leading Kemper to hypothesize a widespread increase in women's testosterone levels as they increase their positions of status and power in society. In short, our bodies respond and change as a result of our experiences and our changing social positions within society.

Clearly, the third part of the above proposition, that biological sex differences make a specific form of *social organization* inevitable, is based on questionable assumptions. In fact, rather than assuming that "biology is (social) destiny," Kemper's and others' research suggests that our biology is shaped, even at times dramatically transformed, by our social experiences. This is not to say that the errors of biological determinism should be replaced by a simplistic social determinism that ignores biology. Instead, R. W. Connell (1995) argues that the old "nature vs. nurture" debates (and, indeed, the social-scientific dichotomy between biological "sex" and cultural "gender") tended to oversimplify and overdichotomize what is really a continuous circuit of "body-reflexive practices" (p. 64).

> Through body-reflexive practices, bodies are addressed by social process and drawn into history, without ceasing to be bodies. . . . Their materiality (including material capacities to engender, to give birth, to give milk, to menstruate, to open, to penetrate, to ejaculate) is not erased, it continues to matter. The *social* process of gender includes childbirth and child care, youth and aging, the pleasures of sport and sex, labour, injury, death from AIDS. (p. 65)

In short, a *social constructionist* perspective parts from biological essentialism by asking the questions, How does our social structure shape our experiences in ways that limit, enable, injure, stimulate, or repress our bodies, thus eliciting a range of possible bodily responses and meanings? And in turn, How do our bodily responses to these socially constructed experiences then enter history and serve to reinforce or challenge the current social order? In the 1990s, biological essentialists, who are attempting to reassert a *scientifically based* view of natural and categorical male-female difference, face three decades of empirical research that reveals a much more complex relationship between social structure and gender. Simply put, it cannot be scientifically demonstrated that biology determines women's and men's social destinies. But Promise Keepers is claiming a higher authority than the scientific method for its essentialist beliefs. Promise Keepers' discourse relies on little or no scientific justification or basis for its essentialist beliefs. Rather than expressing a biological essentialism, Promise Keepers holds to a *biblical essentialism.* Based on faith, rather than on scientific argument, this essentialism allows Promise Keepers' discourse about women to be couched in terms of "respect" for women (in their proper places as mothers, wives, and emotional caretakers of house and home). For example, when John Stoltenberg (1995) attended a 1995 Promise Keepers rally in Texas Stadium, he observed,

> No overtly misogynist slurs—neither from the Promise Keepers stage nor in the milling corridors. Rarely does a presenter even use the word

"woman," much less pronounce a loopy opinion about women's ostensible nature. There is no tit-for-tat accusing of women; nor is there any pop-psych defense of the double standard, as in the secular mega-seller, *Men Are From Mars, Women Are From Venus.* The Promise Keepers' message is much simpler: Men are from God. This obviates the sorts of gender-defender dramas that would-be real men are prone to—contests and put-downs to prove who's got "manhood" and whose is "greater." *God's* manhood is greater—'nuff said. (p. 52)

Thus, although Promise Keepers sometimes draws on modern scientific and social scientific discourses, its biblical essentialism—as opposed to a purely biological essentialism—is largely impervious to empirical refutation.

Taming Men With Patriarchal Bargains

Promise Keepers differs from the mythopoetics in another fundamental way. Whereas we might say that the mythopoetics are antimodern and are seeking to rediscover a premodern, preindustrial essence of manhood, Promise Keepers is attempting to reassert what it sees as a "traditional family" that is based on a God-given division of labor between women (as mothers and domestic caretakers) and men (as providers, protectors, and leaders). In fact, according to Stacey (1990), what is commonly believed to be the traditional family—a married heterosexual couple, with the male performing the paid labor and bringing home a family wage and the female doing the unpaid housework and child care in the home—is actually the modern nuclear family that very briefly achieved prominence as the white middle-class ideal in the post-World War II era. Starting in the 1960s, social conditions (including economic shifts, feminism, and gay and lesbian liberationism) have led to a proliferation of varying family forms and a breakdown in the ideological (and demographic) hegemony of this 1950's middle-class nuclear family. Nevertheless, Promise Keepers seems to be claiming that there is a divine basis for this *Leave It to Beaver* family form.

And whereas mythopoetic discourse on gender and families is, on its surface, apolitical, Promise Keepers has clear political aims. It intends to be a force in confronting and turning back the "downward spiral of morality" that has undermined traditional family values. A Promise Keepers' bumper sticker says it all: "If You Want to Go to Heaven, Take a Right and Go Straight." And it is clearly men who are intended to be at the wheel of this return drive to a mythical pre-feminist and pre-gay liberation era. According to Coakley (1993), McCartney ended the 1992 meeting by proclaiming that "the strongest voice in America is the Christian male" and implored these males "to take the nation for Jesus Christ" (p. 1).

The antifeminist and antigay backlash potential of Promise Keepers is obvious. After all, its most visible leader Bill McCartney "stumped for Colorado's anti-gay Amendment 2 and has been featured at [the militant antiabortion group] Operation Rescue events" (Minkowitz, 1995, p. 67). But it would be a mistake to conclude that political backlash is the only—or even the major—motivating factor for men who join Promise Keepers. Coakley (1993) observes that a dominant theme in the meetings is men's feeling of having lost control:

> . . . control over their children, wives, family lives, themselves, or over the "morally decaying" social worlds in which they lived. The content of the program appealed to men who were searching, fearful, confused, or guilty for their own "sins of insensitivity and ignorance" about how to be responsible fathers, husbands, and "manly men." (p. 1)

For example (Sahagun, 1995), one of the 65,000 men who attended the 1995 Promise Keepers rally in Denver's Mile High Stadium said,

> I came to pick up the seed of belief that can make life better for my family. Right now, my family is like an airplane going down. My wife is the right wing, my children are the left wing. I'm the pilot and we're about to crash. (p. A1)

This assertion of men's responsibility to seize the reigns of family leadership is a key to understanding the appeal of Promise Keepers to men. Beal and Gray's (1995) content analysis of the writings of 60 Promise Keepers leaders revealed that a major theme of Promise Keepers' discourse is the "degradation of egalitarianism" and the reassertion of a natural hierarchy of authority that stretches from God the Father, to His Son, to the father of a family, and finally, down to his wife and children. For instance, Promise Keeper leader Dr. Tony Evans (1994) wrote that "I'm not suggesting that you *ask* for your role back, I'm urging you to *take it back*. . . . There can be no compromise here. If you're going to lead, you must lead. Be sensitive. Listen. Treat the lady gently and lovingly. But *lead!*" (pp. 79-80).

This reassertion of responsible male leadership has not led to a defensive backlash among Christian women. To the contrary, it might very well be the basis for an apparent groundswell of support for Promise Keepers among women in fundamentalist Christian communities. Why is this? Starting in the 1970s and accelerating in the 1980s and 1990s, middle- and lower middle-class families and communities have been profoundly affected by current crisis tendencies in the gender order. Economic shifts and pressures—higher levels of structural unemployment, fewer jobs paying a family wage, rapidly rising costs of housing, and so on—have undermined the likelihood of achieving the male breadwinner and female homemaker middle-class ideal. Moreover, feminism and gay liberationism have undercut the ideological basis for the unquestioned authority of heterosexual males.

Feminism, often viewed as a purely secular movement, has actually had a profound impact on various traditional Judeo-Christian religions. Far from remaining insulated from the feminist revolution of the past 30 years, Catholic nuns (Wittberg, 1989), charismatic Pentecostals (Rose, 1987), African American women church activists (Gilkas, 1985), and Orthodox Jewish women (Kaufman, 1987) have creatively (and selectively) incorporated aspects of feminism into their religions. Similarly, feminist ideals of egalitarian marriages filtered into fundamentalist Christian communities in the 1970s and 1980s (Stacey, 1990; Stacey & Gerard, 1989). But many married fundamentalist Christian women eventually concluded that feminist activism (especially that aimed at reforming individual husbands) had gotten them nowhere. Moreover, the lack of improvement in the economic opportunities and realities for most women left these particular women (especially those who were mothers) economically dependent on men. Thus, the major issue often became not whether the man would agree to clean the toilet but whether he would consistently be a responsible breadwinner, husband, and father. This concern was codified in the 1970s and early 1980s in Phyllis Schlafly's Eagle Forum organization, which viewed the Equal Rights Amendment as a threat to "traditional families" and to the support and protection that these families gave to women. According to Schlafly (1981), if the ERA passed, it would "take away the traditional rights of wives (such as financial support) and give new rights to homosexuals (such as marriage licenses). . . . Laws that say 'husband must support wife' . . . would not be permitted under the ERA" (pp. 24-25).

The combination of men's intransigence in the face of women's pleas for a fair family division of labor, along with women's continued economic dependence, led many women to see the fundamentalist Christian view of "the traditional family" as a secure refuge for themselves and their children, especially if, as an integrated part of a Christian community, men could be tamed into being sober, monogamous, responsible breadwinners and fathers. What has resulted is an attempt to strike what Kandiyoti (1988) calls a new "patriarchal bargain": In return for a domesticated, responsible masculinity, Christian women concede to a clear gendered division of labor (usually with their taking on the vast majority of the housework and child care, even if they are also in the paid labor force) and they concede formal leadership of the family to the man. Thus, there is a great deal of evidence that fundamentalist Christian women are actively supportive of Promise Keepers. Stoltenberg observed at the Texas Promise Keepers rally in 1995 that "several hundred young female volunteers" helped staff the cash registers and merchandising tents and served soft drinks to the press and that "two twentyish women employees of Promise Keepers tell me that they themselves would sure like to meet and marry a man of Promise Keepers caliber some day" (p. 29). Recently, in fact, these women who support Promise Keepers have formed their own organization, "The Promise Reapers."

Potentially, men who join Promise Keepers receive far more than a secure position of authority in their families. Many of these middle-aged men are weary of paying the costs that are attached to trying to live up to the confusing and fragmented modern conceptions of masculinity. Real men, they have learned, have to constantly fight it out among themselves—either literally through violent encounters or through daily battles in workplaces—to prove and then re-prove that they are men. Real men deal with their own hurt and doubts not by talking with ministers, friends, or family members but, instead, through destructive and self-destructive practices, such as drinking too much alcohol, taking other drugs, and/or multiple sexual conquests of women. What a relief it is for many of these men to learn that a real man is simply one who faithfully keeps his promises to be a responsible husband, father, and family breadwinner. In short, like many therapeutic human potential or 12-step programs, Promise Keepers offers these men a clear set of principles and practices through which they may deal with their pain, doubts, and anxieties in ways that are less self-destructive. A man who is secure in his position as a man has no need for alcohol, has no need to destroy his own body or other men's bodies through violence, has no need to resort to sexual promiscuity to prove himself. The sense of relief at being given permission—by thousands of other men, in the masculine environs of a football stadium—to relax one's masculine posturing with one's self and with other men appears to be a great draw for men who attend the Promise Keepers events.

Jesus, after all, has already paid the "costs" of masculinity for these and all men.

So far, no outcome research has been done on these men to determine how much participants' lives and relationships change after they leave Promise Keepers events. As with many therapies and 12-step programs that aim to eliminate destructive behaviors, such as alcohol addiction, it may be that the effects are short-lived, especially if they are not continually followed up with more meetings or groups. It does appear, though, that although the most public face of Promise Keepers is its mass public meetings, a top priority of theirs is to organize and maintain small, local groups of men who continue to meet regularly. In this way, it may come to resemble the kinds of therapeutic movements that have modeled themselves on organizations such as Alcoholics Anonymous.

In sum, Promise Keepers can be viewed, simultaneously, as Christian masculinity therapy in a confusing and anxiety-producing era, as organized and highly politicized antifeminist and antigay backlash, and as a religious intervention through which Christian women hope to secure men's agreement to change their behaviors in ways that are far more dramatic than any amount of "feminist browbeating" was ever able to accomplish. This bargain involves some concrete gains for women; if men keep their "promises," they are likely to become more responsible breadwinners, fathers, and husbands. As Stoltenberg (1995) concludes, "From the point of view of any married woman in their social universe, neither men's talk, nor men's walk ever gets much better than this: Keep your promises to your wife and kids and be a man of your word" (p. 29). But despite these obvious benefits to women, this is still clearly a bargain struck within the rules of a gendered hierarchy that has now been reaffirmed and renaturalized. In short, in the context of the current crisis tendencies in the gender order, Promise Keepers constitutes fundamentalist Christian men's organized agreement to settle into the driver's seat of a new patriarchal bargain with their wives. Indeed, as the wife of one Promise Keeper told him, "If you follow God, I'll follow you anywhere" (Sahagun, 1995, p. A1).

CHAPTER 3

The Limits of "The Male Sex Role"

The Men's Liberation
and Men's Rights Movements

Male liberation seeks to aid in destroying the sex role stereotypes that regard "being a man" and "being a woman" as statuses that must be achieved through proper behavior. . . . If men cannot play freely, neither can they freely cry, be gentle, nor show weakness—because these are "feminine," not "masculine." But a fuller concept of humanity recognizes that all men and women are potentially strong and weak and active and passive; and these human characteristics are not the province of one sex.

—*Jack Sawyer (1970, p. 1)*

What [the men's liberation movement] really amounts to is just more of the same old male supremacist complaint that women are really nags and bitches—the power behind the throne—henpecking their men into subservience. The new twist is their attack, sometimes subtle and sometimes not, on the women's liberation movement they usually claim to support.

—*Carol Hanisch (1975, p. 72)*

In the early 1970s as the women's liberation movement was exploding onto the social scene, most men responded with either hostility or stunned silence. But from the onset, mostly centered around colleges and universities, some men were starting to engage themselves with feminist ideas and politics and to ask a potentially subversive question: What does this all have to do with us?

The Men's Liberation Movement

One of U.S. men's first organized responses to the reemergence of feminism in the early 1970s was the origination of "men's liberation" consciousness-raising groups and newsletters. As early as 1970, women's liberation gatherings, such as the March 8 teach-in at Northwestern University, were including workshops on "The Male Liberation Movement" (Sawyer, 1970). The first book length texts that appeared— Warren Farrell's (1974) *The Liberated Man*, Marc Feigen Fasteau's (1974) *The Male Machine*, and Jack Nichols's (1975) *Men's Liberation*—all acknowledged that sexism had been a problem for women and that feminism was a necessary social movement to address gender inequities, but they also stressed the equally important high costs of "the male sex role" to men. Men's liberation was especially focused on the ways in which socialization oriented boys and men toward competition and public success, while stunting their emotional and relational capacities. Thus, a major attraction of men's liberation was the permission it gave to men to expand their definitions of manhood to include the emotional expression, "It's okay to cry."

The Limits of Sex
Role Theory

Many of the early leading advocates of men's liberation were psychologists who were drawing on sex role theory that had developed in the 1950s, 1960s, and 1970s (e.g., Hartley, 1959). Sex role theory had progressive implications in demonstrating that masculinity and femininity were socially scripted behaviors rather than biologically based male and female essences. For instance, psychologist Robert Brannon's (1976) highly influential article summarized the four main rules of the male script: "No Sissy Stuff," "Be a Big Wheel," "Be a Sturdy Oak," and "Give 'Em Hell" (pp. 1-45). Not only did Brannon demonstrate how this script is socially constructed, he also argued that the male sex role was oppressive to women and harmful to men. Psychologist Joseph Pleck arguably took sex role theory to its most subversive and progressive limits (Pleck, 1976, 1982; Pleck & Sawyer, 1974). Significantly, it was Pleck's more sociological and historical works that revealed most clearly the power dynamics of social relations. His 1974/1995 article, "Men's Power With Women, Other Men, and in Society," still stands as one of the most insightful and often reprinted contributions to understanding the social construction of masculinity in the United States. In this article, Pleck attempted to come to grips with a paradoxical reality: Men hold institutional power in patriarchal societies, but most men don't feel very powerful. Pleck argued that the male sex role that was necessary for men to compete and win in public life was emotionally and psychologically impoverished, leading men to feel that women had "expressive power" and "masculinity-validating power" over them. As Pleck (1974/1995) explained it,

> Men's dependence on women's power to express men's emotions and to validate men's masculinity has placed heavy burdens on women. By and large, these are not powers over men that women have wanted to hold. These are powers that men have handed over to women, by defining the male role as being emotionally cool and inexpressive and as being ultimately validated by heterosexual success. (p. 7)

Despite the subversive intentions of its most sophisticated adherents, such as Brannon and Pleck, sex role theory had built-in limitations and dangers, and these limits are revealed in the developing discourse and practice of men's liberation. As Connell (1987), Stacey and Thorne (1985), and others have argued, role theory tends to rely on individualistic and psychological examinations of gendered attitudes and personalities, rather than to develop institutional analyses of gender relations that necessarily take power as a central focus of concern. The language of sex role theory—for instance, the notion that women and men learn "reciprocal roles" that prepare men to handle the "instrumental" and women the "expressive" tasks of life—allowed some men's liberationists to begin to argue in the early 1970s that men and women were "equally oppressed" by sexism. In this usage, the concept of "oppression" was depoliticized and seemed to refer only to a general condition faced by everyone in a sexist society. Critics of sex role theory pointed out that we do not speak of "race roles" or "class roles" but rather of race and class *relations*. Similarly, a theoretical focus on *gender relations*, they asserted, would help us to see oppression as a relational concept; for there to be an oppressed group, there must, in turn, be an oppressor group.[1] Sex role theory allowed men's liberationists to sidestep this politicized language of gender relations in favor of a falsely symmetrical call for women's and men's liberation from oppressive sex roles. In short, early men's liberationists tended to give equal analytical weight to the "costs" and to the "privileges" attached to "the traditional male and female roles" (see Figure 3.1).

   The resulting sense of gender symmetry—the belief that sex roles hurt both women *and* men, and thus that "there's something in feminism for men too"—was one of the major attractions of men's liberation for some men. Indeed, this sense of gender symmetry in men's liberation resulted in the enlistment of some men as allies in liberal struggles, such as the attempt to pass the Equal Rights Amendment. But gender

FIGURE 3.1

The Terrain of the Politics of Masculinities: The Men's Liberation and Men's Rights Movements

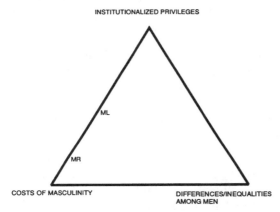

INSTITUTIONALIZED PRIVILEGES

ML

MR

COSTS OF MASCULINITY   DIFFERENCES/INEQUALITIES
                              AMONG MEN

ML = Men's Liberation Movement
MR = Men's Rights Movement

symmetry also constituted one of the major limitations and dangers of men's liberation, and Warren Farrell's views are prime examples of this.

In the mid- to late 1970s, Farrell was known as the most public "male feminist" in the United States. He was an early member of the National Organization for Women, an outspoken advocate of the ERA, and his workshops in the early 1970s included activities such as "beauty contests for men," which were aimed at raising men's consciousness about the oppressive ways that sexual objectification turned women into "pieces of meat" to be consumed by men. Despite these innovative activities, some feminists were wary—others openly critical—of Farrell's tendency to downplay the institutionalized privileges that men still enjoyed at women's expense. Instead of an analysis of patriarchal institutions, Farrell's mostly psychological analysis emphasized how socially learned reciprocal sex roles tended to hurt both women and men. For instance, in response to feminist criticisms of the effects on women of being construed as "sex objects," Farrell (1974) posited an equally negative effect on men in being construed as "success objects":

> Women become objects not only of the male sex drive but of a man's need to use women to prove himself a man to other men. . . . However, the more a man has to "produce pussy" the more he molds himself into

the object he thinks will attract the woman. . . . A woman becomes a sex object as a man becomes a success object. (pp. 48-49)

Some feminists greeted the arrival of the men's liberation movement with critical skepticism. For instance, Nancy Henley wrote in a 1970 newsletter that men's liberation groups often focus on

the bitchiness, rather than the oppression of women: under the present system, women are taught to be bitches, manipulating men, etc. If we off the system, women will be tolerable and men will therefore be liberated. Such discussions are not only inadequate and misleading but also dangerous, because they ignore the political context that is necessary to understand women's oppression. (p. 1)

Similarly, in the 1975 radical feminist collection *Redstockings,* Carol Hanisch (1975) warned of the "anti-woman, anti-women's liberation" impulse in men's liberation. Hanisch asserted that the purely psychological (rather than institutional) focus of the analysis, as well as the positing of a false symmetry between the oppression of women and men by socially imposed sex roles, held the danger of defusing the radical potential of feminism and turning "sensitive men" into anti-feminist advocates of "men's rights" (p. 72). As we shall see later, in the discussion of men's rights advocates, this is precisely what happened to Warren Farrell in the 1980s and 1990s.

The False Universalization of "Men"

In addition to its reliance on sex role theory, men's liberation had a second limitation: a tendency to falsely universalize the experiences of white, middle-class, college-educated, heterosexual men as those of all men. Most of the early men's liberationist texts were written by heterosexual men who recognized the ways in which homophobia hurt all men but rarely focused on the experiences and lives of gay men (Nardi, 1994). Moreover, mirroring problems inherent in liberal feminists' false universalization of "women" (Baca Zinn et al., 1986), men's liberationist texts, such as Marc Gerzon's (1982) *A Choice of Heroes,* tended unblinkingly to speak of "men's problems" with work, success, relationships, and health as though all men were white, college-educated professionals. This tendency to assume professional class status as the norm was mirrored in much of the early academic writing on masculinity. For instance, the section on "men and work" in Pleck and Sawyer's (1974) groundbreaking collection, *Men and Masculinity,* contained articles about stockbrokers, doctors, academics, and executives but nothing on blue-collar men or unemployed men. As Clatterbaugh (1990) points out, "the owning/professional/managerial class" (p. 113) constitutes only about 15% of the population, so this focus on the experience of class-privileged men leaves out the experiences of the great majority. By ignoring the institutionalized racial and class constraints faced by black, Latino, Asian, working-class, and poor men, men's liberationists could preoccupy themselves with the "lethal aspects of the male role" and the "burden of the breadwinner role" but avoided the issue of their own positions of privilege within race, class, and gendered hierarchies. As a result, calls for "changing masculinity" were reduced to simplistic arguments for greater lifestyle choices, a wider range of acceptable emotional expression, and opportunities for self-actualization for (privileged) men. As Ehrenreich (1983) observed, this men's liberation-ist focus on self-actualization was articulated in the individualist lan-guage of an ascendant middle-class human potential movement that gave middle-class men "permission" to abandon the responsibilities of the male breadwinner role. Liberated men, it seemed, could now "get in touch with their feelings" and still feel good about their status, power, and privilege over others.

The Men's Rights Movement

Whereas men's liberationists gave equal weight to the limitations and oppression imposed on women and men and viewed feminism as a movement for human liberation, men's rights advocates emphasized far more the costs of masculinity to men.[2] Early men's rights texts, such as Herb Goldberg's (1976) *The Hazards of Being Male*, were similar to early men's liberationist texts in that they tended to argue that both women and men have been hurt by sexism, but the men's rights texts differed in the fact that they tended to place much greater emphasis on the costs of masculinity than on the problems faced by women. By the late 1970s and early 1980s, men's rights discourse had all but eliminated the gender symmetry of men's liberation from their discourse, in favor of a more overt and angry antifeminist backlash. Feminism was viewed as a plot to cover up the reality that it is actually *women* who have the power and *men* who are most oppressed by current gender arrange-ments. Men's shorter life-span, health problems, military conscription, and divorce and custody laws were used as evidence of men's oppres-sion. From the point of view of some men's rights advocates (e.g.,

Goldberg, 1979), women's liberation was a movement that was forcing men to receive "the worst of both worlds."

Men's rights discourse began to take form in various organizations. In 1977, Men's Rights, Incorporated, an organization that focused on legal and policy reform, was formed; in 1980, the Coalition of Free Men, an organization with a wide agenda of change, inspired by Herb Goldberg, was formed; and also in 1980, these two organizations joined with several fathers' rights organizations to form an umbrella organization, the National Congress for Men.

By the late 1970s and early 1980s, men's rights advocates were claiming that men are the true victims of prostitution, pornography, dating rituals, sexist media conventions, divorce settlements, false rape accusations, sexual harassment, and even domestic violence. Whereas men's liberation discourse—despite its limits—often relies on solid social scientific research, men's rights discourse often displays a blatant disregard for widely accepted sociological, economic, and psychological studies. Instead, men's rights discourse has tended to rely on anecdotal stories, combined with a few highly questionable studies, that provide an emotionally charged basis for the development of an ideology of male victimization. Take, for instance, the issue of spousal violence. Men's rights activists have argued that feminist ideology and men's shame have combined to cover up massive numbers of men in families who are physically abused by women (Logan, 1985) and murdered by women (Panghorn, 1985). But in a recent survey of the research on this topic, Jack Straton (1994) concluded that the much-touted "battered husband syndrome" is a myth. U.S. National Crime Survey data show that only between 3% and 4% of interspousal violence involves attacks on men by their female partners, and 92% of those who seek medical care from a private physician for injuries received in a spousal assault are women (Schwartz, 1987). For every 46 women hospitalized for injuries received in a spousal assault, only one man is hospitalized (Saunders, 1988). Many of the studies that compare spousal violence rates do not include violence that occurs after spousal separation and divorce, yet "these account for 75.9% of spouse-on-spouse assaults, with a male perpetrator 93.3% of the time" (Straton, 1994, p. 80). This is not to say that men are not injured and killed as a result of violence. But the vast majority of men's injuries that result from violence and 87% of the murders of men are perpetrated by other men (Straton, 1994).

It is instructive to examine the slippage in the discourse from the symmetrical mid-1970s men's liberationist language of "equal oppressions" faced by women and men to an angry antifeminist men's rights language of male victimization in the late 1970s and 1980s. This slippage was, in fact, built into the language of men's liberation from the start, and this is best illustrated by the words of some men's rights leaders—several of whom were early men's liberationists. For instance, M. Adams, writing in 1985, said that in the early 1970s, he had been hopeful that feminism might lead to human liberation but was disappointed to find that the women's movement was interested only in "unilateral liberation" for women and did not address the problem of male oppression. To prove his point, he did some research on sex role attitudes and reported that the results "showed that men were truly the victims of prejudiced thought, discriminatory attitudes, in general, oppression. I felt that I had won the theoretical argument with feminism." But when nobody would accept his perspective, he laments, "I began to consciously hate women" (p. 14). By the end of the 1970s, he had become an outspoken member of the "Free Men," and when he told some women at a party that he understands oppression from his own experience, "They didn't have the slightest idea what I meant. I laughed out loud at the expressions on their faces. I didn't bother to explain. The movement was coming. . . . They'd understand soon enough" (Adams, 1985, p. 14).

Several themes in Adams's story are repeated in much of the biographical discourse of men's rights activists (see Baumli, 1985; Farrell, 1993): first, the claim of having been an early and ardent supporter of (liberal) feminism in the hopes that it would free women and men from the shackles of sexism; second, the use of the language of sex role theory that equates sexist thoughts and attitudes with oppression without discussing gendered institutional arrangements and intergroup relations; third, a sense of hurt and outrage when women don't agree that "men's issues" are symmetrical with those faced by women; and fourth, an enthusiastic embrace of an angry and aggressive antifeminist men's rights discourse and practice. Former men's liberation leader and current men's rights spokesperson, Warren Farrell, is the best known example of a man who has traversed this path, as the shift in tone of the titles of his books indicate. In 1974, it was *The Liberated Man;* by 1993, it was *The Myth of Male Power.* Farrell has helped take men's rights discourse to a new level, now claiming that in fact it is women who have the power and men who are powerless. For instance, in response to women's having fought back against sexual harassment in workplaces, Farrell now claims that, in fact, it is male employers who are disempowered and victimized by their secretaries' "miniskirt power, cleavage power, and flirtation power" (Farrell, 1993, p. 129).

Perhaps it is true that some women learn to use their sexuality to manipulate male employers. But is this a sign of women's power over men? Of course not, as should be clear by a cursory glance at sexual harassment claims that often result in the woman being (formally or informally) forced to leave her job and the male perpetrator's hand being slapped. A woman who uses sexual manipulation to get by in the workplace has drawn on what she has learned is her one available resource to better her condition, in a context in which she had no direct access to political, economic, and legal institutional power. But men's rights leaders such as Richard Haddad even seem to have an answer to this point. Haddad (1985) states that men really don't have a "monopoly on power" in public life—they are simply "over-represented in decision-making positions in . . . government and industry" (p. 282).

The antifeminist backlash tendencies in the discourse of men's rights advocates are clearly evident, but these activists are not arguing for a return to patriarchal arrangements and "traditional masculinity." To the contrary, men's rights advocates are critical of the ways masculinity has entrapped, limited, and harmed men, and they want to reconstruct a masculinity that is more healthful, peaceful, and nurturing. But importantly, they do not see feminism as the way to improve men's lives. To the contrary, they disagree with the feminist contention that men enjoy institutionalized privileges. To men's rights advocates, the social construction of masculinity has primarily resulted in costs *to men* (see Figure 3.1), and they believe therefore that a men's movement is needed to fight for men's rights vis-à-vis women.

"Fathers' Rights" and the Realities of Men's Family Labor

Although men's rights organizations have a broad agenda of change, the issue of "fathers' rights" has been their most successful rallying point, by far. Arendell's (1992, 1995) research suggests why some divorced fathers are attracted to the men's rights agenda. In her study of recently divorced fathers, Arendell found that many of the divorced fathers that she studied responded to "the stresses and turmoil of the divorce" by developing a "masculinist discourse on divorce." This discourse included as its main themes: (a) the belief that father absence is a viable "strategy of action, the objective of which is to control situations of conflict and tension and emotional states," and (b) the development of "a rhetoric of rights through which relationships, actions, and emotions were framed and defined" (Arendell, 1992, p. 582). Many divorced fathers, who may also feel that the courts have discriminated against them in child custody rulings simply because they are men, have found men's rights organizations to be powerful vehicles through which to focus their anger and sense of injustice. Men's rights leader Rich Doyle (1985) sums up this fathers' rights anger:

> Divorce courts are frequently like slaughter-houses, with about as much compassion and talent. They function as collection agencies for lawyer fees, however outrageous, stealing children and extorting money from men in ways blatantly unconstitutional. . . . Men are regarded as mere guests in their own homes, evictable any time at the whims of wives and judges. Men are driven from home and children against their wills; then when unable to stretch paychecks far enough to support two households are termed "runaway fathers." Contrary to all principles of justice, men are thrown into prison for inability to pay alimony and support, however unreasonable or unfair the "Obligation." (p. 166)

Fathers' rights discourse has attempted, with some success, to co-opt the liberal feminist rhetoric of gender "equality" and "rights" to forge a campaign that aims to alter laws related to divorce and child custody. But what fathers' rights discourse rarely includes is a discussion of fathers' responsibilities to children *before* divorces. Research on contemporary heterosexual families indicates that many young men are more inclined than were their fathers to help out with housework and child care, but most of them still see these tasks as belonging primarily to their wives (Machung, 1989; Sidel, 1990). Despite the cultural image of the "new fatherhood" and some modest increases in paternal involvement by men, the vast majority of child care, especially of infants, is still performed by women (Coltrane, 1995; Hochschild, 1989; La Rossa, 1988; Lewis, 1986; Russell, 1983).

Why does men's stated desire to participate in parenting so rarely translate into substantially increased involvement? Lynne Segal (1990) argues that today's fathers may (correctly) fear that increased parental involvement will translate into a loss of their power over women and a loss of a competitive edge in their workplaces. But she also argues that increased paternal involvement in child care will not become a widespread reality unless and until the structural preconditions—especially economic equality for women—exist. Indeed, Rosanna Hertz (1986) found in her study of upper-middle-class dual career families that a more egalitarian division of family labor sometimes developed as a rational (and constantly negotiated) response to a need to maintain his career, her career, and the family. In other words, career and pay equality for women were structural preconditions for the development of equality between husbands and wives in the family.

However, Hertz notes two reasons why this is a very limited and flawed "equality." First, Hertz's sample of dual career families in which the women and the men made roughly the same amount of money is still extremely atypical. In two-income families, the husband is far more likely to have the higher income. Women are far more likely than men to have part-time jobs, and among full-time workers, women still earn about $.69 to the male's dollar and are commonly relegated to lower-paid, lower-status, dead-end jobs (Blum, 1991; Reskin & Padavic, 1994; Reskin & Roos, 1990). As a result, most women are not in the structural position to be able to bargain with their husbands for more egalitarian divisions of labor in the home. As Hochschild's (1989) research demonstrates, middle-class women's struggles for equity in the home are often met by their husbands' "quiet resistance," which sometimes lasts for years. Such a woman is left with the choice of either leaving the relationship (and suffering not only the emotional upheaval but also the downward mobility, often into poverty, that commonly follows divorce) or capitulating to the man and quietly working her "second shift" of family labor.

Second, Hertz observes that the roughly egalitarian family division of labor among some upper-middle-class dual career couples is severely shaken when a child is born into the family. Initially, new mothers are more likely than fathers to put their careers "on hold." But eventually, many resume their careers, as the child care and much of the home labor is performed by low-paid employees, almost always women and often immigrant women and/or women of color. The construction of the dual career couple's "gender equality" is thus premised on the family's privileged position within a larger structure of social inequality. In other words, some of the upper-middle-class woman's gender oppression is, in effect, bought off with her class privilege, while the man is let off the hook from his obligation to fully participate in child care and housework. The upper-middle-class father is likely to be more involved with his children today than his father was with him, and this will likely enrich his life. But given the fact that the day-to-day and moment-to-moment care and nurturance of his children are still likely to be performed by a woman (his wife and/or a hired, lower-class woman), "the contemporary revalorization of fatherhood has enabled many men to have the best of both worlds" (Segal, 1990, p. 58). The cultural image of the "new father" has given the middle-class father license to choose to enjoy the emotional fruits of parenting, but his position of class and gender privilege allow him the resources with which he can buy or negotiate his way out of the majority of "second shift" labor.

Recent research on men's contributions to household labor sheds light on the differences between more and less privileged men. Contrary to the popular belief that it is white, professional-class men who are on the cutting edge of a movement toward more egalitarian relations with women, research on men's household labor time indicates that Latino men do the most housework, followed by black men, with white men doing the least. Shelton and John's (1993) conclusion that Latino men "spend more time on 'female-typed' tasks than other men" (p. 145) is supported by Hondagneu-Sotelo's (1992) research that shows Mexican immigrant men moving toward more egalitarian relations with their wives. These findings are fascinating, especially given the way the "macho" stereotype is often projected onto Latino men (Hondagneu-Sotelo & Messner, 1994).

Fathers' rights activists, who are predominantly white and middle- or working-class, tend to ignore how work and family institutional relations benefit them, both before and after divorces. Instead, they focus entirely on the economic and emotional costs that are attached to these masculine privileges—among them, the common legal assumption after a divorce, that children are better off spending the majority of their time with their mothers. Whereas very few of these fathers ever contributed anywhere near 50% of the child care *before* the divorce, they passionately argue for the right to joint custody—or, in some cases, sole custody—of their children *after* the divorce (Coltrane & Hickman, 1992). Bertoia and Drakich (1995) conclude from their interviews with fathers' rights activists that "the rhetoric of fathers' rights gives the illusion of equality, but in essence, the demands are to continue the practice of inequality in postdivorce but now with legal sanction" (p. 252).

The language of sex role symmetry, created by liberal feminists, thus supplied the building blocks for an ultimately antifeminist men's rights discourse. By the late 1970s, men's liberation, as a self-conscious liberal feminist movement, was gone. To be sure, some of the ideas of men's liberation—especially the belief that women and men are both hurt and limited by narrow "sex roles"—filtered into the culture in general and continued to be reflected in practices such as feminist family therapy. But the men's liberation movement had fragmented in essentially two directions. The first, as we have seen, was the men's rights movement. The second, as we shall see in the next chapter, was a profeminist movement that largely abandoned the language of sex roles in favor of a more politicized language of gender relations.

Notes

1. Mirra Komarovsky (1992), one of the founders of sex role theory, recently has argued that critics are wrong to conclude that sex role theory is inherently individualistic and conservative. She argues that when properly situated within a historical and macrosociological analysis of patriarchy, "role analysis affords an exceptionally productive link between macro- and micro-level perspectives" (p. 306). Whether she is correct or not, in what follows, I will argue that role theory, when disconnected from macro-level analyses of patriarchy, does offer a useful language for a decidedly depoliticized analysis of gender that can serve as an instrument of antifeminist backlash.

2. In the mid-1970s there was a tentative and uneasy alliance between some of the activists in the men's rights movement with the originators of the profeminist men's movement and its organization, the National Organization for Changing Men (NOCM, later changed to NOMAS). By 1977, it was clear that the men's rights and profeminist men were in opposing camps, and men's rights leaders were no longer invited to NOCM national conferences (see Brannon, 1981-1982).

CHAPTER 4

Profeminist Engagements

Radical and Socialist
Feminist Men's Movements

Many men have said that their male hurt and their male pain
would be tempered if only men would learn to cry more, or feel
more, or trust other men more, or have better sex. Many such men
would prefer to make self-interested emotional accommodations
rather than moral commitment. . . . But I believe that there are a few
genital males who are persuaded that what is wrong with the
culture is its sexist injustice and that what is wrong with their lives
is their complicity in it.

—*John Stoltenberg (1977, p. 81)*

For socialist men especially, it is necessary to challenge a prevailing
left-wing sectarianism which relegates questions of personal and
family life to peripheral status—as "women's issues." Feminists
and gays have themselves criticized the chauvinism on the left. . . .
Both groups have initiated a far-reaching debate with a
male-dominated socialist tradition. It is vital that "men against
sexism" begin to take a constructive position within this
debate—supporting the attention to personal experience and the
critique of socialist dogmatism. . . . The challenge to socialist men is
to understand masculinity as a social problem—and thus to work
together for a non-sexist socialist society.

—*Andrew Tolson (1977, pp. 145-146)*

In the early 1970s, a radical feminist male discourse and practice was born
in the same welter of activity that bred men's liberation. In fact, in these
early days, the boundary lines between these tendencies were not clearly
drawn at all. In the spring of 1971, a collective of four radical men in
Berkeley, California, put out the first issue of *Brother: A Male Liberation
Newspaper*. By the fall of 1971, the third issue of *Brother* now had a different
subtitle: *A Forum for Men Against Sexism*. As I demonstrated in the previous chapter, men's liberation ultimately gave rise to a conservative,

antifeminist men's rights movement. But there were other men who were less impressed with the liberal, middle-class feminism of Betty Friedan, Warren Farrell, and NOW and were far more influenced by radical feminism and by the radical impulses in the fledgling gay and lesbian liberation movement. Like the early men's liberationists, these radical men focused a great deal on the "costs" of masculinity, as well as on the institutional privileges afforded to all men under patriarchy. For example, in 1971, one of the first expressions of this new men's consciousness was published in a 60-page book called *Unbecoming Men*, a product of a profeminist men's consciousness-raising group. The men in the group critically examined their own lives in light of the feminist dictum that "the personal is political." As a result, the book was startlingly personal—for instance, the men in the book discussed their own masturbation habits and the pain of having been considered a "sissy" as an adolescent. To be sure, this can be seen as a plus in early men's groups, in light of New Left "radical" men's tendency to revel in radical theories that abstracted away from the personal and enabled them to ignore their own gender (and other) privileges in their own progressive and revolutionary organizations. On the other hand, the lack of an analytical framework within which to discuss these personal feelings tended to leave much of the early men's radical profeminist discourse at the level of guilty personal interrogation rather than critical social analysis (Men's Consciousness-Raising Group, 1971).

By the early to mid-1970s, as feminist women began to criticize men's liberation, radical profeminist men moved their discourse more clearly in the direction of de-emphasizing the costs of masculinity and emphasizing the ways that all men derive power and privilege within patriarchal society, a shift that was foreshadowed by the 1971 change in the subtitle of *Brother*. Thus, as Figure 4.1 shows, I place radical profeminist men in the upper "power and privileges" corner of the terrain of the politics of masculinities.

By the mid-1970s, radical men's profeminism had begun to take organizational form, as indicated in the formation of the East Bay Men's Center (EBMC) in Berkeley. An excerpt from the EBMC's "Statement on Rape" (reported in Snodgrass, 1977) illustrates how far the radicals' antipatriarchal discourse had parted from the sex role symmetry of men's liberation discourse:

> Sexism is a system where one sex has power and privilege over another. In a society, such as ours, where men dominate women, this system can be called male supremacy. We believe violent rape to be the extreme form of sexism and male supremacy. (p. 137)

FIGURE 4.1

The Terrain of the Politics of Masculinities: Radical Feminist and Socialist Feminist Men's Movements

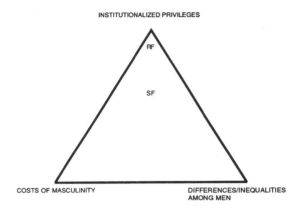

INSTITUTIONALIZED PRIVILEGES

COSTS OF MASCULINITY   DIFFERENCES/INEQUALITIES
                                        AMONG MEN

RF = Radical Feminist Men
SF = Socialist Feminist Men

The EBMC's statement contains three themes that came to characterize radical feminist men's discourse. First, sexism is seen as a *system* of male supremacy—patriarchy—rather than simply as a set of attitudes or values that can be unlearned. Second, in this system, "men as a group" *dominate* women. In other words, men are viewed as a category of people who systematically oppress—and benefit from the oppression of—another category of people, women. Third, rape and other forms of sexual violence are viewed as "the extreme form" and the major locus of male domination of women. This perspective was presented in a clear and analytically sophisticated way for the first time in a 1977 collection of articles called *For Men Against Sexism*, edited by Jon Snodgrass. Several articles in the book soundly criticized the men's liberation movement. In one article, titled "Warren the Success Object," Don Andersen (1977) wrote that while reading Warren Farrell's book, *The Liberated Man*,

> I sometimes got the feeling that businessmen are finally reacting to the threat of the women's movement, and that Farrell is here to take the bite out of it and to demonstrate how women can be compromised. (p. 147)

In place of men's liberation, these radical men created a men's politics of "antisexist practice," focused mainly on sexual violence issues. In particular, Jack Litewka's (1977) article, "The Socialized Penis," a powerful synthesis of critical self-reflection and radical feminist analysis of the social construction of patriarchal heterosexuality, eventually became one of the most widely reprinted and discussed articles on male sexuality. Litewka first described three troubling recent experiences with difficulty getting or keeping an erection when making love to a woman. Instead of seeing this purely as his own "personal trouble," Litewka examined his experiences in light of the social construction of the patriarchal male heterosexual script. This three-part sexual script, which boys and men learn from the media (especially from pornography) and from other males, essentially trains men to relate to women—and to their own bodies—in prescribed ways that are oppressive to women and ultimately dehumanizing to men:

1. *Objectification:* From a very young age, males are taught by everyone to objectify females (except Mom?). They generalize the female, in an almost platonic sense. This generalized woman is a concept, a lump sum, a thing, an object, a non-individualized category. The female is always "other" . . .

2. *Fixation:* Part of the male sexual initiation is learning to fixate on portions of the female's anatomy: at first, breasts, and later, that hidden unknown quantity, the vagina. . . . Because of the way we are socialized, erection follows fixation or occurs in a situation in which fixation plays a role. . . . We learn that we can *will* an erection without a woman being near us. And because it is pleasurable (and, at first, astounding), because it gives us assurance that we are male, we create erections out of our imagination, by merely objectifying a female of our choice [and] fixating on the parts of her body that excite. . . .

3. *Conquest:* To conquer is a highly valued skill in our society. We are taught to alter the enemy into nothingness, to convert the bear into a stuffed head or rug, to gain power and rule. . . . In sexual matters, the male conquers when he succeeds in reducing the female from a being to a thing and achieves some level of sexual gratification. . . . Conquest logically (ahem) follows Objectification and Fixation. (pp. 23-24)

Through this three-stage process, Litewka argues, men learn to relate to women as objects to be fixated on and conquered, rather than as full human beings. The line between this form of "normal sex" and rape is pretty thin. And the way that this process intertwines erotic pleasure with power and conquest over a devalued female object also alienates men from their own bodily pleasures. As a result, according to Litewka, men like himself often experience "sexual dysfunctions" when their anxieties are raised when confronted by a female sexual partner who demands to be seen and treated as a fully human, empowered subject (rather than a fragmented, disempowered object).

Snodgrass's collection of works by men against sexism was also one of the first places in which the work of John Stoltenberg was made more widely available. Heavily influenced by the ideas of Andrea Dworkin and other radical feminists, Stoltenberg used a powerfully moving speaking style and insightful analytic capacity to become a major leader in radical feminist men's politics. Stoltenberg founded Men Against Pornography in New York City and was Chair of the NOMAS Task Group on Pornography. The titles of his books, such as *Refusing to Be a Man* (1989), speak to the radical feminist politics of renunciation. This is no move to *reform* masculinity but to do away with gender distinction (and thus, inequality) altogether. Stoltenberg's categorical view of men as oppressors and women as the oppressed and his nearly constant focus on male sexuality and sexual violence as the major locus of patriarchal oppression reveal the major strengths and the limitations of radical feminist men's discourse and politics.

First, the view of men as categorically privileged at women's expense and the view of one cluster of issues (sexuality, sexual violence) as the major link in patriarchy provide an analytic simplicity through which an otherwise complicated politics of antisexist practice might be concretely forged. Buttressed with this analysis, profeminist men began to link up with the feminist rape crisis movement, the antipornography movement, and the battered women's movement to attempt to stop these problems at their sources—men's violence. In the United States, radical feminist men organized mainly at a local level. In 1979, RAVEN (Rape and Violence Ends Now) was organized in St. Louis, Missouri, and EMERGE: A Men's Counseling Service on Domestic Violence was formed in Boston, Massachusetts. In California, also in 1979, the Oakland Men's Project was launched with the slogan, "Men's Work: To Stop Male Violence" (Kivel, 1992). These groups still exist and have inspired and germinated groups in other cities that offer therapeutic interventions with men who batter, and they engage in antiviolence education. In Canada, men's antiviolence efforts have had a more national impact, especially with the impressive success of the "White Ribbon Campaign"

(Kaufman, 1993). Begun in response to the 1989 murders of women at the University of Montreal, the campaign gained the support of a large number of Canadian men who were (at least symbolically, by wearing a white ribbon on the anniversary of the massacre) stating a commitment to end violence against women. Through the campaign, discussions of violence against women and moves by men to contribute to ending the violence have broadened far beyond what the antisexist men's movement in the United States has been able to imagine possible.

But the sense of clarity and focus that radical feminist male discourse gives to political organizing is also its major limiting factor as well, for two reasons. First, the almost exclusive focus on men's shared privileges and almost total disregard for the costs of masculinity contribute to a politics of guilt in which men's major reason for challenging patriarchy might appear to be altruism toward women. As Connell (1995) puts it, although this may be a noble reason for activism, "How can a politics whose main theme is anger toward men serve to mobilize men broadly?" (p. 221). Second, although the universalizing claims about "male power" make for moving oratory that arouses a passion for justice among a few men who commit themselves to stop the violence against women, a discourse that posits gender as the fundamental dividing line of power in the world does not accurately reflect the complexity of the real world. Social class, racial and ethnic, sexual, and other systems of power intersect with gender in ways that make progressive political organizing a tremendously complex reality. Just as the universalization of "women" tends to obliterate the differences, power differentials, and inequities among women (Baca Zinn et al., 1986; Segal, 1987), so too does the radical feminist universalization of "men" create a context in which a profeminist men's movement obliterates the different (and perhaps at times, opposing) experiences, views, and interests of poor men, blue-collar men, and men of color (Brod, 1983-1984). Radical feminist men's discourse has not entirely obliterated the recognition of difference among men. In fact, the "gay-straight" binary has been fundamental to the development of radical thought on men and masculinity. But through this lens, gay issues are, first and foremost, examined in terms of radical feminist *women's* standpoint. For example, many gay men have been openly opposed to the feminist antipornography movement because they have experienced gay pornography as a liberating medium in a heterosexist society that has denied them pleasure, community, and identity (Clark, 1990; Tucker, 1990). In response to this, John Stoltenberg (1988) argues that gay pornography is simply another part of the oppressive apparatus that eroticizes violence. Gays who are "in the propornography movement" are not advocating freedom, Stoltenberg asserts; to the contrary, they are merely "having the hots for sex discrimination" (p. 11). This refusal to adopt (even tentatively) the different standpoints of oppressed groups of men and put them into play with feminist standpoints leads to the near impossibility of radical feminist men's discourse and practice leading to coalition-building politics.

A final, related limitation of radical feminist men's discourse is its reductionist focus on "male sexual violence" as the locus of men's oppression over women. The analysis of male sexuality borders on a categorical essentialism that often leads to a politics of individual guilt. And the focus on sexual violence as *the* issue tends to lead activists away from engagement with structured inequalities within social institutions, such as workplaces, families, and the state. The irony of this, as Segal (1987, 1994) and others have argued, is that in the search for an issue (such as pornography) that links all women, radical feminists have ignored or marginalized issues such as pay equity, day care, parental leave, and welfare reform—that are often the major concerns of working women, mothers, poor women, and women of color. Radical feminist men have followed suit, thus leading to a politics of disengagement with issues that have the greatest potential for coalition building.

Socialist Feminist Men

Socialist feminism, which began to develop in the mid-1970s as a blending of some radical feminist and Marxist concepts and strategies (Eisenstein, 1979; Hartmann, 1976), informed some impressive attempts at antisexist organizing efforts in workplaces in Australia (Gray, 1987) and Great Britain (Tolson, 1977). In the United States, despite some efforts by socialist feminists to organize women workers (Hansen, 1986; Sealander & Smith, 1986), and despite a highly influential presence in organizations such as the Democratic Socialists of America (DSA), socialist feminism never developed a significant activist base outside of academia (Hansen & Philipson, 1990). Despite this limited base, socialist feminists have been an important presence in much of the U.S. profeminist men's movement (especially NOMAS) and in its academic wing, the Men's Studies Association, which sponsors a scholarly journal called *masculinities*. As a result, the curriculum of a growing number of college courses on men and masculinities is highly influenced by socialist feminist thought (Brod, 1987; Kimmel, 1987a; Kimmel & Messner, 1989, 1995). The discourse of socialist feminism, highly influenced by Marxist structuralism, parted dramatically from the psychologism and individualism of men's liberationism. Socialist feminists viewed masculinity not as a personal style or internalized attitude but as part of a structure of power. But socialist feminism also parted significantly from radical feminism, in that class inequalities were given at least as much analytic importance as gender inequalities. Thus, socialist feminists were among the first to call for an examination of inequalities among men, rather than relying on a simplistic and falsely universalized definition of "men" as an undifferentiated sex class. This was (and still is) a very difficult and tricky task, but socialist feminists set about attempting to strike a balance between an analysis of the ways that patriarchy benefits all men and the ways in which social class inequalities benefit some men at the expense of other men and women. This primary focus on men's power and privilege within patriarchy, with an additional focus on class inequalities among men and the concomitant fact that certain groups of men pay different kinds of "costs" within patriarchal capitalism, explains my placement of socialist feminist men closer to the center of the terrain of the politics of masculinities (see Figure 4.1). Andrew Tolson's (1977) book, *The Limits of Masculinity*, was among the first attempts to grapple with these ideas. Tolson made several important contributions to the then-emergent sociology of masculinities. First, he pressed socialist men to confront feminist insights concerning the importance of personal life and sexual relations. But he refused to define "masculinity" entirely—or even mainly—in terms of sexuality, as many radical feminists appeared to be doing. Instead, Tolson illuminated the importance of work as central to men's identities and positions within industrial capitalism. And significantly, Tolson began to delineate how men's different experiences and interests, grounded in their different— often oppositional—positions in workplaces and in the larger political economy, led to the social construction of a "working-class masculinity" that was in some ways distinct from "middle-class masculinity." Working from examples of his native England where class distinctions have been more acknowledged than in the United States, Tolson (1977) argues that working-class and middle-class men both "have inherited the patriarchal culture of the past and both experience the erosion of patriarchal privilege by capitalist expansion" (p. 81). But for working-class men, the breadwinner role offers a "paradox of masculinity." On the one hand, the wage bolsters a man's "public presence" and gives him a material basis for power within his family. On the other hand, the daily experience of work "poses a constant threat to masculinity" (p. 48), due to the fact that every day, the manual worker faces an "immediate alienation (his product is 'objectified' against him) and a direct, personal humiliation (constant confrontation with authority)" (pp. 58-59). In short, waged work *simultaneously supports and undermines* working-class men's masculine status. This paradox leads to two interrelated outcomes. First, in a context of a lack of institutional power, exaggerated styles of masculine bravado become more pronounced. Second,

> Because of the often brutal and unpredictable nature of the work, the worker is directly dependent on "masculine" compensations and in some situations patriarchal aspects of working-class culture may even be potentially subversive. A male chauvinism of the shop-floor is a way of asserting collective control and, sometimes, sabotaging the production process itself. (p. 59)

In short, one common way that male manual workers bond together is to talk and joke about their male managers in disparaging ways. The managers are positioned as feminized "paper pushers" who do not do "real men's work." Through this process, the men on the shop floor use misogyny and homophobia to position themselves as the "real men." This sort of masculine posturing and bonding may result in feelings of masculine power in a context in which these men have very little institutional power (see Collinson, 1988; Peña, 1991). In effect, this kind of masculinity (relying as it does on an assertion of superiority over women and over feminized males) serves as a "cultural bribe," where the working-class man's "social commitment is won at the price of his independence—for which he is offered the empty promise of 'manhood' " (Tolson, 1977, p. 46).

Middle-class men, according to Tolson (1977), face different paradoxes in their relationship to work and families. Until fairly recently, professional and managerial class work for men involved a moral commitment to a career and an "ethic of service" to "Empire, the Nation, or at a local level, the 'community,' 'civic pride' " (p. 82). But in the post-World War II era, the rise of large bureaucracies and an increasingly insecure and shifting economy has "stripped away the idealistic cloak surrounding middle-class work and has revealed, for the first time, its naked insecurity" (p. 86). The resulting alienation and "crisis of confidence" among middle-class men has led to two distinct reactions. One pattern is the development of a "cynically detached business personality." Here, men of the professional and managerial class who lack any moral foundation for their work simply decide to pursue their work as a game in which the goal is gaining status, power, and wealth. This sort of masculine cynicism seemed to reach a new level in the 1980s, as some yuppies got rich quick by selling illegal junk bonds and drove new BMWs with bumper stickers that read, "He Who Dies With the Most Toys Wins!" A second response to the middle-class crisis of confidence, according to Tolson (1977), was the development of "the myth of domesticity." In short, many middle-aged, professional-class men became disillusioned with their work and turned to family life:

> For the disillusioned male careerist, this myth of "domesticity" has become his last remaining source of support. Against the anxiety of his professional "crisis of confidence" he will still make domestic plans, direct operations, project himself into the future. As husband and father, he is the *subject* of an ideology to which his wife and children are the *objects*—of his concern, his protection, his authority. And his focal position is maintained by his continuing *economic* power. (p. 95)

Tolson points out that a major strain in professional men's retreat to domesticity as a haven and as a place where they could revive their sense of patriarchal authority was the fact that this is a time in history when middle-class *women* are moving into the public world of higher education and careers. In both a symbolic sense and in a very concrete way, men who are returning to the home in hopes of having their masculinity affirmed may be literally passing their wives who are going out the door into public life.

Tolson's socialist feminist approach offered new and increasingly complex ways to think about masculinity, not as a singular male sex role (as men's liberationists thought of it) or as a singular dominant sex class (as radical feminists saw it). Rather, masculinity began to appear as a multiple reality that is constructed in relation to women *and* in relation to men's varying and opposing class positions vis-à-vis other men. In the next decade, largely influenced by Tolson and other socialist feminists, scholars such as Harry Brod (1987), R. W. Connell (1987), and Lynne Segal (1990) began to posit the now widely accepted notion that at any given time there are multiple masculinities—some hegemonic, some marginalized, some subordinated. In short, socialist feminist examinations of gender were among the first to part with the universalizing tendencies of men's liberationists, men's rights advocates, and radical feminist men. The feminist impulse demonstrated that men benefit, as a group, from patriarchy, but the socialist impulse insisted that class inequalities among men distribute patriarchy's benefits—and its costs—very unequally.

Socialist feminism involved far more than a deconstruction of "masculinity." Feminist insights led to a radical rethinking and expansion of several key Marxist concepts. For instance, narrow Marxian notions of "labor" were criticized for contributing to the invisibility of women's work, especially unpaid labor in the home. Socialist feminism's expansion of the concept of labor to include unpaid labor and its problematizing of the gendered public and domestic split laid the potential groundwork for a new politics of work and family, which simultaneously challenged the hegemony of capitalist rationality, of the male family wage, of housework and child care as privatized women's work, and of sexualized power relations in workplaces. Concretely, in the United States, socialist feminism informed the rise of "comparable worth" as a collective strategy to overcome structured pay inequities, as opposed to "affirmative action," a strategy that relies on individual mobility out of underpaid and undervalued occupational ghettos (Blum, 1991). And socialist feminist discourse also has contributed to the call for a government family policy—ideally similar to those of social democracies, such as Sweden—which, in effect, would involve the state in breaking down gendered divisions of labor in and between workplaces and families (Sidel, 1986). It is this emphasis on the necessity to change *institutions* such as workplaces and the state, rather than simply appealing to individual men to change their sexist attitudes and practices, that socialist feminism makes its most important contribution (Segal, 1990, p. 309).

Some of the problems and limitations of socialist feminism have always been internal to it as a troubled (and mostly theoretical) "marriage" between what some have claimed are only partially compatible feminist and Marxist concepts (Hartmann, 1981). And there has always been the dangerous tendency of Marxist categories eclipsing feminist concepts, thus reverting back to a prefeminist era when "the woman question" was always relegated by male Marxist leaders to an issue that would be dealt with "after the revolution" (Stacey, 1983). A final problem internal to socialist feminism is grounded in the Marxian tendency toward an economic reductionism that tends to view race as a superstructural manifestation of class relations and sexuality as an invisible nonissue. Thus, in socialist feminist discourse, "inequalities among men" risks being reduced to *class* (not racial and ethnic, sexual, or other) inequalities among men, and the "costs of masculinity" risks being reduced to costs related to poverty and work alienation but not to racism or homophobia.

Despite its internal limitations, through the early 1980s, socialist feminist discourse demonstrated the greatest potential among feminist discourses to develop a balanced understanding of the structured privileges, costs, and inequalities among men (and as we shall see in subsequent chapters, this tendency in socialist feminism has been picked up and developed in the 1980s and 1990s by many feminist women of color). The inability of this theoretical discourse to translate into effective political action is related, in part, to the above internal problems of socialist feminism, but I would argue that it has more to do with the political-economic context of the United States. In short, although socialist feminist theory informs a view of the state as an arena in which to fight for issues such as pay equity, day care, and parental leave, the two-party system in the United States has always precluded the development of a radical base in national politics and leaves little room for anything but the most limited liberal feminist discourse on individual rights. This stands in sharp contrast to parliamentary democracies, such as those of Australia, Canada, Great Britain, France, and the Scandinavian countries, which have institutional space within state politics for the articulation of labor, socialist, feminist, Green, and other progressive politics (Franzway, Court, & Connell, 1989). Second, the proportion of U.S. workers—especially women workers—who are unionized is very low and continues to shrink. Moreover, unions in the United States are fairly weak and thus most are not in a position to push for radical reforms, such as comparable worth or paid family leave (Sidel, 1986).

These internal and external barriers may have relegated socialist feminism to the margins of politics in the United States, but socialist feminist discourse has had a broadening influence on internal debates within the U.S. profeminist men's movement. Whereas liberal feminism tends to focus on the articulation of individual rights and individual "growth" (an articulation that tends disproportionately to benefit class-privileged women and men), and radical feminism tends to take the body, sexuality, and violence as central to its analysis of power, socialist feminism tends to focus more centrally on production, work relations, and work/family relations (Clatterbaugh, 1990). As a result of this focus, socialist feminist men in organizations such as NOMAS have raised issues related to the "class basis and bias" of the profeminist men's movement and the importance of examining men's varying experiences in workplaces and in the economy (Brod, 1983-1984). Socialist feminist men also have brought important insights to the debates about men, pornography, and violence against women. For instance, Harry Brod has been the most systematic in employing and adapting Marxist categories to analyze issues raised first by radical feminists, including those related to sexuality and violence. Brod does not dispute the radical feminist claims concerning the links between pornography and violent male domination of women. But he adapts Marxian concepts to argue that men, as consumers of pornography, experience a bodily alienation and a loss of sexual subjectivity that results in a denial of satisfaction of men's human desires. In short, commercial pornography simultaneously benefits and hurts men (Brod, 1984). Michael Kimmel, another profeminist activist highly influenced by socialist feminist thought, also has engaged in the pornography debates and has come to somewhat different conclusions. Kimmel (1990) agrees that we should be critical of the eroticization of violence against women but also argues that (a) there is no established empirical link between viewing pornography and acts of violence against women—sexual fantasy, in short, is not the same as reality; (b) sexual repression itself is dangerous and oppressive, and the antipornography movement may contribute to increased state repression not only of sexual minorities but of sexual pleasure in general; (c) some groups, such as gay men, find pornography liberating. The differences between Brod's and Kimmel's perspectives (though perhaps not as wide as I have portrayed them) raise a key question for all profeminist men. In short, *with which feminism shall we ally ourselves?* The "feminism" in Brod's socialist feminist analysis of pornography leans toward the radical feminist antipornography views of Andrea Dworkin and John Stoltenberg, whereas the "feminism" in Kimmel's perspective is more clearly linked to the socialist feminist "proerotica, anticensorship" perspec tive of feminists such as Ann Snitow (Snitow, Stansell, & Thompson, 1983), Ellen Willis (1983), and Lynne Segal (1994). Whether one agrees with the antipornography feminists or the proerotica feminists on the centrality of pornography and rape in men's overall power over women, it seems clear that radical feminists tend to *reduce* explanations of women's oppression to this issue, whereas socialist feminists tend to *connect* women's need for sexual empowerment and safety to issues of larger institutional struggles. As British socialist feminist Lynne Segal (1987) put it,

> Struggles in and around the state and work around trade unions . . . are of equal importance to sexual politics and ideology if only because they are inevitably linked: economically independent women find it easier to make choices, to leave brutal men, assert a lesbian lifestyle if they want to, and decide if, when and how they wish to mother. (p. 244)

Socialist feminism, then, promises to broaden the terms of feminist debates about men and masculinity beyond individualistic discussions of sexual politics to more broadly political discussions of collective movements, made up of women and men who are working together to transform existing social institutions.

CHAPTER 5

Racial and Sexual Identity Politics

*Racialized Masculinity Politics
and Gay Male Liberation*

It is patently clear that the central concerns of Black men are not about relinquishing male privilege or forging new concepts of androgyny or sex-role egalitarianism. They must first and foremost deal with the issue of survival. It is not that they have abused the privileges accruing to men, but that they have never been given the opportunity to realize even the minimal perquisites of manhood—life-sustaining employment and the ability to support a family. . . . We should realize that the more these legitimate aspirations to manhood are retarded, the greater the tendency will be to assert them in other areas.

—*Robert Staples (1982, p. 13)*

We who are gay-identified have a unique opportunity to see through the facades that pass for masculinity in our culture. . . . [However], the post-Stonewall gay-identified male . . . affects the poses of machismo partly because he is overreacting to the pre-Stonewall limp-wrist image, an image once connected to effeminacy and drag. He is emphatic about being a conventional male because masculinism is so highly valued. He is likely to say: "I am a man. I'm not a drag queen. People think gays are effeminate, but I'm not. I can be just as masculine as the next guy." Little does he know that the "next guy" is trying to keep up appearances too.

—*Jack Nichols (1977, p. 330)*

Over the past 12 years, I have taught a course called Men and Masculinity, first at a state-funded university and now at a private university. Consistently, the course draws between 80% and 90% women. Regarding the few men who do find their way to this course, I have noticed a consistent pattern: Disproportionately, they identify as members of racial and ethnic minority groups, as members of sexual minority groups, or both. Of course, this pattern says something about the men who are *not* taking these courses. Perhaps most men who identify as white and heterosexual feel that to sign up for such a course would make a public statement that they have some problem with their own sense of manhood. Or perhaps most of them simply have not thought much about issues related to gender, sexual orientation, or race (Messner, 1993b). By contrast, young men of color, gay or bisexual men, or men who are struggling to define their sexual identities have often faced a lifetime of influences that call their basic sense of manhood into question. This leads some men from these groups to question and sometimes even to overtly challenge dominant social conceptions of masculinity. Other men from these groups respond by even more assertively and aggressively staking claims to hegemonic masculinity.

It is this paradoxical tendency in the politics of masculinities among these marginalized and subordinated groups of men that I will explore in this chapter. First, I will look at what I call "racialized masculinity politics." By that, I mean organized political discourses and practices that take up questions of manhood but usually within what is assumed to be a larger, more fundamental framework of racial politics. Although I tie in some discussion of Asian American men and Latino men, my discussion of racialized masculinity politics is focused far more on African American men. There are two reasons for this. First, African Americans represent the largest racial and ethnic minority group in the United States; second, there is simply far more social scientific literature on African American men than on other groups of men of color. After discussing racialized masculinity politics, I will conclude the chapter with a discussion of the paradoxical masculinity politics of gay male liberation.

Racialized Masculinity Politics

On October 16, 1995, an estimated crowd of 837,000 people—nearly all of them African American males—converged on the Capitol in Washington, D.C., for the "Million Man March (MMM)."[1] The men of the MMM reflected a wide range of religious and political backgrounds and interests, and they tended disproportionately to be middle- and upper-middle-class.[2] Journalist Herb Boyd (1995) wrote that the MMM

was a special moment of rare epiphany for men who have endured the effects of chattel slavery, racism and humiliation, who have been pushed to the margins of society, bruised by an array of negative stereotypes, alienated from affection and respect, and, for the most part, rendered invisible. (p. 12)

The MMM reflects a growing sense of urgency among African American males that they need to respond collectively to a major crisis that is destroying black communities and families. And increasingly, young black males are seen as most at risk. Indeed, since the mid-1980s, respected academics and educators have increasingly employed apocalyptic language to describe the problems and dilemmas facing young black males in the United States. Consider some recent titles: "Surviving the Institutional Decimation of Black Males" (Franklin, 1987); *Young, Black, and Male in America: An Endangered Species* (Gibbs, 1988); *Countering the Conspiracy to Destroy Black Boys* (Kunjufu, 1985).

Are things really that bad for black males today? The answer is not entirely simple. After all, a black middle class of educated professionals has expanded dramatically in the wake of the civil rights movement of the 1950s and 1960s. But behind this visible progress lies the reality that socioeconomic conditions have actually deteriorated for the vast majority of African Americans. Black male unemployment rates are more than twice those of white males, and estimates of unemployment rates for black male youths approach 60% (Taylor, 1994). A disproportionately high number of black males are homeless (Jones & Christmas, 1994) and are infected with the HIV virus (Bowser, 1994). Homicide rates among black males more than doubled between 1960 and 1988 (Gibbs, 1994), and in general, violence has become a way of life among many young black males (Canada, 1995). Black males are dramatically overrepresented in the criminal justice system: In 1989, about one in four of all black males between the ages of 20 and 29 was either in prison, in jail, on probation, or on parole. Part of this is due to bias in the criminal justice system: Black males, who make up 40% of all those condemned on death row, are far more likely to be condemned to death than white males who have committed similar crimes. And there are more black males—about half a million—who are in prison or jail than are enrolled in higher education (Mauer, 1994). Indeed, schools in many predominantly black communities have deteriorated in recent decades, and dropout rates among young black males are at crisis proportions—between 40% and 70% in cities such as New York, Chicago, Philadelphia, and Detroit (Taylor, 1994).

As a result, young black males are increasingly described as alienated, angry, endangered, embittered, embattled, and lacking hope for
the future (Gibbs, 1988, 1994). Young black males today are living with
the legacy of 20-plus years of deindustrialization, rising joblessness,
declining inner-city schools, and conservative politicians who preach
"just say no" to drugs and gangs, whereas the only things worth saying
"yes" to crumble (Wilson, 1987). As Elijah Anderson (1990) observes,
the decline of solid blue-collar jobs for black males and the suburban
flight of much of the black middle class have left young inner-city black
males with few "old heads," a term that refers to adult male community
leaders who have traditionally taught young males the value of hard
work, family support, and community responsibility. Today, Anderson
observes, these traditional "old heads" have been replaced by the more
respected "new heads"—young street toughs and drug dealers with
wads of cash and, often, with guns. The Million Man March was
organized to respond to this crisis and to project a positive image of
responsible adult black males who will "stand up" to care for families
and communities and to mentor young black males.

Race, Sexuality, and Respect

Several years ago, when I was interviewing former male athletes
about their lives, I asked these men to discuss their motivations for
working so hard to be successful athletes (Messner, 1992). An interesting
pattern emerged. The black and Latino men all discussed their motivations in terms of the importance of achieving "respect," but the white
men never raised that issue unless I raised it first. How do we explain
this difference? Part of the answer has to do with the dominant negative
public images of black men and other men of color. Stuart Alan Clarke
(1991) has asserted that American society is obsessed with images of
"black men misbehaving." Young black males are all too aware of this.
For instance, about 5 years ago at the University of Southern California,
where I teach, there were several attempted rapes in a campus parking
structure by a man who was described as a "tall, thin, thirtyish, black
male." One of my black male students, twentyish, short, and stout told
me that he was put up against the wall and frisked by police on campus.
He told me that "all of us black guys know to walk around campus with
books and briefcases, dressed like students or we'll be hassled by the
police." Despite their status as college students, they knew and had
directly experienced the reality that black males, especially in public
life, are far more likely to be *sus*pected than *re*spected. African American

males' shared knowledge of the increasingly limited structure of opportunity that they face and their day-to-day experience of Americans' obsession with "black men misbehaving"—especially our obsession with black men's *sexual* "misbehaviors"—go a long way toward explaining the high levels of skepticism toward the legal system in African American communities—and the support among significant segments of African American communities for convicted rapist Mike Tyson and for O. J. Simpson when he was accused (and acquitted) of murder (Gordon, 1995).

Historically, sexuality has been an especially salient part of the racial oppression of black women and men. For instance, as Angela Davis (1981) has pointed out, the historical construction of "the myth of the black male rapist" served as a key ideological construct in the continued race and class subordination of black males in the post-Civil War years. When men who had been slaves attempted to move into the paid labor force, they were seen as a threat by many white men, who used terror tactics such as lynchings to enforce a color bar in the workforce. Some people, including many northern whites, responded to this terror with outrage. So instead of simply lynching black men, the white terrorists invoked the image of an aggressively sexualized black male who threatened white womanhood: Now, black men were lynched *and* castrated. Staples (1986) observes that "between 1884 and 1900, over 2500 Black men were lynched, most of whom were falsely accused of sexual interest in white women" (p. 4). Once the image of the black male threat was sexualized, most of the outrage that had been expressed earlier by white liberals evaporated and was replaced by silence. We can see in this example how the imposition of an animalistic, sexualized image onto black men served as a means of control within a system of race and class stratification that had been destabilized by the legal emancipation of slaves. Lynne Segal (1990) observes that, a century later, this is still very much the case:

> To this day, although 50 per cent of men convicted for rape in the Southern states are white, over 90 per cent of men executed for rape are Black (mostly accused of raping white women). No white man has ever been executed for raping a Black woman. (p. 178)

Whereas the "myth of the black male rapist" serves as a means of holding the black man down economically, there is evidence that it simultaneously constructs a deeply sexualized psychological fear of black men in white men's minds. Paul Hoch (1979), employing a psychoanalytic perspective, suggests that white males have projected the image of the oversexed "black beast" onto black males as a means of sublimating our own repressed sexual desires. As a result, the potential unleashing of black male sexuality tends to trigger white men's most deeply repressed fears. In the 1950s, psychiatrist Franz Fanon used a word association test to measure the fears of his white patients. Nearly 60% of the responses to the word *Negro* were terms such as *biology, penis, strong, athletic, potent, savage, animal, evil,* and *sin,* thus revealing, perhaps, whites' association of "blackness" with sexualized, dangerous, evil bodies (Fanon, 1970, p. 118). More recently, psychologists Chester Pierce and Wesley Profit (1994), in their research on racial group dynamics, observed that white males reveal a deep fear of black males by tending not "to reveal weakness, inferiority, uncertainty, or anxiety in front of Black males" (p. 169). Their research has also revealed that "white men in the presence of Black men spend many more seconds covering their genitalia than when they are by themselves" (p. 169).

Whereas we can see how the image of animalistic sexual aggression was imposed on black males as a means of controlling their full participation in public life, by contrast, Asian American males have been stereotyped as feminized *de*sexualized males (Fung, 1996). For example, journalist Ben Fong-Torres (1995) has asked why there are no Asian anchor*men* on television news, while there are numerous highly visible Asian female anchors. He argues that historically—and especially grounded in images that arose in the United States' wars against Japan and Vietnam—Asian women have been stereotyped as "exotic," ultra-feminine, heterosexually desirable, and thus nonthreatening. On the other hand, Asian men have been stereotyped as small, wimpy, unattractive, yet highly intelligent in "unscrupulous" and untrustworthy ways. Asian men are thus viewed as precisely the kind of people you would not trust to be presenting the news. In short, whereas black men are limited through an imagery of oversexed bodies with low intelligence, Asian men are limited through an imagery of undersexed bodies with an overabundance of intelligence that is too often used in manipulative ways.

Are these sexualized racial images simply imposed on men of color? Clearly, men of color sometimes resist these damaging images. At other times, they passively accept the stereotypes that are imposed on them, and at still other times, they actively take up these stereotypes and attempt to redefine and manipulate them for their own benefit. For instance, leaders of the late 1960s and early 1970s Black Power Movement, such as Eldridge Cleaver and Stokely Carmichael, purposefully embodied and displayed an aggressively heterosexual masculine persona as a way of waging psychological warfare against their white male oppressors. Carmichael was "the nightmare America had been dreading—the Black man seizing his manhood, the Black man as sexual, virile, strong, tough, and dangerous" (Wallace, 1978, p. 60). More recently, black men's embodiment and stylized public display of highly sexualized and aggressive postures have been described as "cool pose." As Richard Majors (1995) describes it,

> Cool Pose, manifested by the aggressive life style, is also an aggressive assertion of masculinity. It emphatically says, "White man, this is my turf. You can't match me here." Though he may be impotent in the political and corporate world, the Black man demonstrates his potency in athletic competition, entertainment and the pulpit with a verve that borders on the spectacular. Through the virtuosity of a performance, he tips the socially imbalanced scales in his favor. "See me, touch me, hear me, but, white man, you can't copy me." This is the subliminal message which Black males signify in their oftentimes flamboyant performance. Cool Pose, then, becomes the cultural signature for Black males. Being cool is a unique response to adverse social, political and economic conditions. Cool provides inner strength, stability, and confidence. . . . The poses and postures of cool guard, preserve and protect his pride, dignity and respect. (p. 83)

Though Majors highlights cool pose's therapeutic value and its role as symbolic resistance to racism, he also notes its sometimes self-destructive dangers. In my own view, cool pose is an example of creative agency in resistance to racism—but it is an agency that too often uncritically accepts, valorizes, and employs the dominant cultural definitions of aggressively heterosexualized masculinity as a weapon. Clearly, the imposition, manipulation, and contestation of heterosexualized images and identities has become a key battleground in struggles between men in race and class hierarchies (note Majors's point that the primary audience for black men's cool performances is imagined to be the "white man"). Though they may be less visible, women play key roles in these sexualized battles within intermale dominance hierarchies— either as (white) virgins to be "protected" or "threatened" or as sexualized and debased objects through which to stake a claim to "manhood." Women's sexual agency or pleasure is rarely considered in these phallic wars between men.

Although cool pose may be a therapeutic means of survival for many black males, its focus on individual style and performance does not address the need for collective action to confront the structural and institutional forces that have systematically oppressed black people for centuries. That level of action is the province of mass social movements, not of individual style.

Contradictions of Racialized Masculinity Politics

The Million Man March is often viewed as a mass expression of racially based identity politics (Daniels, 1996). But I see the MMM also as an excellent example of the contradictions and tensions inherent in the dominant expressions of *racialized masculinity politics* among African American men and more generally among men of color in the United States. The MMM mission statement (Karenga, 1995) was couched in a broad language that was aimed at

> reaffirming the best values of our social justice tradition which require respect for the dignity and rights of the human person, economic justice, meaningful political participation, shared power, cultural integrity, mutual respect for all peoples, and uncompromising resistance to social forces and structures which deny or limit these. (p. 3)

For this social justice to be attained, the mission statement asserted, black men now need to "stand up" and assume a "new and expanded responsibility without denying or minimizing the equal rights, role and responsibility of Black women in the life and struggle of our people" (Karenga, 1995, p. 3). The wording of this mission statement likely expresses the compromises that needed to be reached by the coalition that organized the MMM. Certainly the language of "equal rights" for black women expresses more of a liberal feminist view, whereas the language of the "role and responsibility" of black women likely expresses the more conservative and essentialist views of leaders such as Louis Farrakhan of the Nation of Islam. In the weeks and months preceding and following the MMM, much of the critical dialogue within African American communities revolved around this question: When we ask black men to "stand up" *as men*, are we asking them to stand up hand-in-hand with women, as equals, or are we asking them to stand up above women and children as black patriarchs? Many well-known black women activists and leaders, including Rosa Parks and Maya Angelou, were strongly supportive of the MMM; others, such as Angela

Davis, Marcia Gillespie, and Charlene Mitchell, expressed concern that the March would exacerbate a "division between African American women and men" (Boyd, 1995, p. 13).

A gender division of labor was clearly and intentionally built into the organization of the event itself. Along with the very public event of the Million Man March, a less publicized "Day of Absence" was planned. The Day of Absence called on "all Black people to stay away from work, from school, from businesses, and from places of entertainment and sports and turn inward and focus on the themes of atonement, reconciliation and responsibility in our lives and struggle" (Karenga, 1995, p. 9). The mission statement declared that just as men were to be in the leadership of the MMM, "women are in the leadership of the Day of Absence" (Karenga, 1995, p. 8). As a symbolic statement of the organizers' views of the roles of black men and women, this gender symmetry spoke volumes: Black men were to publicly "stand up," en masse, whereas black women were to retreat from public life and "turn inward" in prayer, meditation or "in groups of family and friends at home or . . . places of worship" (p. 9). In short, a gendered public and domestic split was symbolically enacted as a solution to the crisis of black families and communities.

Clearly, not all participants in the MMM agreed with all aspects of the mission statement. For instance, Robert Allen (1995), a senior editor of *The Black Scholar* and a member of the Oakland Men's Project, a community education organization that deals with sexism, racism, and male violence, wrote that calling for black men to "stand up for justice" was not the same as calling for men to reclaim "their 'rightful' place as head of the family. . . . Black men are not the enemies of women, but the ideology of male supremacy is the enemy of us all" (p. 24). As I will discuss in Chapter 6, this sort of profeminist voice among men of color—though extremely important—is still quite rare. The dominant theme in the discourse of racialized masculinity politics in the United States has tended primarily to be concerned with the need to strongly assert men of color's rightful claims to "manhood" as a means of resisting white men's racial (and often also, simultaneously, social class) domination of men of color. Thus, as you can see in Figure 5.1, I position the dominant expression of the politics of men of color near the lower right "differences and inequalities among men" corner of the terrain of the politics of masculinities.

This is not to say that there are no tensions, disagreements, and contradictions *within* racialized masculinity discourses. In fact, in what

FIGURE 5.1

The Terrain of the Politics of Masculinities: Racialized Masculinity Politics and the Gay Liberation Movement

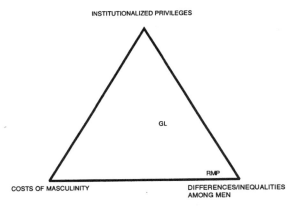

GL = Gay Liberation Movement
RMP = Racialized Masculinity Politics

follows, I will argue that there are two dominant views coexisting in an uneasy tension and permeating much of the discourse of racialized masculinity politics in the United States:

■ *Conservative essentialism.* Advocates of this view believe that there are symmetrical "roles" that women and men should play and that these roles reflect natural differences between women and men. The essentialism underlying these beliefs is often based in fundamentalist Christian or Islamic religious beliefs but may also be intertwined with biological essentialism. In this view, racism has "emasculated" men of color, who now need to fight for respect and social equality by strongly asserting a "manhood" that is decidedly patriarchal. Feminism, in this view, is a white middle-class movement that threatens to divide and further destroy people of color's families and communities.

■ *Radical reductionism.* Advocates of this view tend to see gender as socially constructed and tend to believe that equality between women and men is desirable. However, they tend to see the struggle against race and class oppression as being of primary importance and gender oppression as a distorted, secondary effect of race and class oppression. In other words, the struggle for social justice is *reduced* to a struggle against race and class oppression. In this view, women and men should work together against race and class oppression and not be distracted by "bourgeois feminism" that might divide, rather than unite, women and men.

I will next turn to a critical examination of these two tendencies.

Conservative Essentialism

In 1965, Daniel Patrick Moynihan's *The Negro Family: The Case for National Action* stimulated tremendous debate about the causes and consequences of black poverty and other related problems. Rather than pointing to the effect of generations of slavery and institutionalized racism, Moynihan argued that blacks suffered from a pathological and "abnormal family structure." In short, black women were doing better in school, were moving into white-collar occupations in great numbers, and were controlling families through a "matriarchal" system of power. By contrast, black men were falling behind in education and in the workplace. Thus emasculated, they were not allowed to play their normal roles as family leaders and breadwinners (Moynihan, 1965).

Moynihan's report was soundly and widely criticized—especially by African Americans—for "blaming the victims" of poverty rather than pointing the finger at institutionalized racism. But ironically, many of Moynihan's core assumptions about gender and families appear to have been uncritically taken up by movement leaders within African American communities. Eldridge Cleaver (1965), for instance, expressed the essence of the black power movement in his proclamation, "We shall have our manhood." In this manner, the fight against racism came to be defined largely as a battle for the rights and dignity of black men to be *men*. Black women, of course, were viewed as integral to this struggle, but it was often expected of them that they remain in the background, doing the necessary support work as men occupied the public "frontlines" of the movement. Implicit in this gendered division of labor was an essentialist assumption that restoring black males to their proper positions of leadership necessarily represented the interests of black families and communities as a whole. From this point of view, feminism threatened to introduce divisive ideas into the anti-racism struggle. This perspective was summed up in 1971 by Nathan Hare:

> This is the era of liberation, and because it is the era of liberation, the Black man will be able to bring the woman along in our common struggle, so that we will not need a Black women's liberation movement. In the struggle to reassert our Black manhood, we must sidestep

the trap of turning against our women and they, in retaliation, turning against us. The Black woman is, can be, the Black man's helper, and undying collaborator, standing up with him, beside her man. (p. 33)

In this passage, Hare defines the struggle against racism as a "common struggle" of black men and women, and it is this commonality that makes a separate women's liberation movement unnecessary. But "the struggle" is also clearly defined as an effort to "reassert our Black manhood," and black women are positioned as "the Black man's helper." The explicit gendered hierarchy that was built into this "common struggle" led some black feminist women to argue that the struggle against racism needed to be strongly infused with a feminist impulse (e.g., Wallace, 1978). But for essentialist black leaders, feminism was part of the problem, not the solution. "Feminism," according to Hare and Hare (1984),

allowed the white man to keep his act together while he further alienated and distorted and confused Black male/female relationships. This trend in turn impacts upon and pulverizes the Black male's relationships with the Black woman which are now compounded by the ambiguities and rationalizations resulting from the ideals and rhetoric of an anti-male, even anti-maternal, white feminism. (p. 154)

In fact, Hare and Hare suggest that the current plight of the black male as "an endangered species" is ignored due to "the white race's unilateral feminist agenda and the goals of unisexualization." Hare and Hare also see gay and lesbian liberation as a mechanism through which the white race's "liberal-radical-moderate-establishment-coalition" is destroying black families:

White teachers infiltrate Black child centers, nurseries and primary schools, compelling Black boys to play with blonde dolls in the name of progress; and they are determined to leave no path to a clear and coherent masculine identity. In every way, unisexualization and homosexuality are lionized, produced, promoted and inevitable. (p. 66)

These sorts of themes—that there are essential roles that men and women should play in healthy families and communities; that feminism and gay liberation have been imposed on black communities by the white power structure to further erode black manhood and disrupt black families; that the antiracism movement needs therefore to foreground black men's "standing up" as strong family and community leaders—are threads that run through conservative essentialist racialized masculinity politics. Though I call them "conservative," I want to emphasize that, in some limited ways, these political discourses help to empower many men of color and their families to survive in a racist society. But in terms of the political terrain that I am examining in this book, they are conservative because their antiracist impulses are based on a reassertion of a hierarchical gendered division of labor. And their explicitly antifeminist, antigay, and (often) procapitalist discourse tends strongly to preclude the building of broad alliances with other progressive groups. In fact, the conservative sexual, gender, and economic discourse of many of the leaders of the Million Man March—for instance, Louis Farrakhan—positions this strain of racialized masculinity politics closer to the heart of American conservatism than to progressive groups. For instance, the call for less reliance on government welfare and more self-determination echoes conservative George Gilder's (1981) claim that government welfare programs may have feminized black men and thus made them less competitive in the free market:

> In their present pass, Black men need . . . an increased stress on aggressiveness, competitiveness, and the drive to get ahead. . . . It is the greater aggressiveness of men, biologically determined but statistically incalculable, that accounts for much of their earnings superiority. (p. 137)

In contrast to Gilder's biological essentialism, Farrakhan's discourse is based on religious essentialism, but the outcome may be remarkably similar. "Farrakhan," stated NAACP leader Dan Rojas, "has been striking themes that would have comforted the late [Elijah] Muhammad [the founder of the Nation of Islam who died in 1975] and would today please any diehard Republican: family values, self-reliance, self-discipline, frugality, sobriety, civility, and enterprise" (as cited in Boyd, 1995, p. 16).

Radical Reductionism

Radical structural analyses of the lives of men of color have been more critical of sexism than have their conservative essentialist counterparts. For instance, in an insightful analysis of Chicano men and masculinity, Baca Zinn (1982) argued that in societies where the standards of hegemonic masculinity are that a man should control resources (and other people), men who do not have access to these standards of masculinity thus tend to react with displays of toughness, bravado, or "hombre." Marginalized and subordinated men, in other words, tend to overtly display exaggerated embodiments and verbalizations of masculinity that can be read as a desire to express power over others within a context of relative powerlessness. Recent literature on Latino men in the United States has illuminated some of the limitations of the race and class reductionism that often underlie this kind of observation. According to the dominant cultural stereotype, Latino men's "machismo" is supposedly characterized by extreme verbal and bodily expressions of aggression toward other men, frequent drunkenness, and sexual aggression and dominance expressed toward normally "submissive" Latinos. Manuel Peña's (1991) research on the workplace culture of male undocumented Mexican immigrant agricultural workers suggests that there is a great deal of truth to this stereotype. Peña examined the male Mexican immigrant's participation in *charritas coloradas* (red jokes) that characterize the basis of the workplace culture. The most common basis of humor in the *charritas* is sexualized "sadism toward women and symbolic threats of sodomy toward other males" (Paredes, 1966, p. 121).

On the surface, Peña (1991) argues, the constant "half-serious, half-playful duels" among the men, as well as the images of sexually debased "perverted wenches" and "treacherous women" in the *charritas*, would appear to support the stereotype of the male Mexican immigrant group as being characterized by a high level of aggressive masculine posturing and shared antagonisms and hatred directed toward women. But rather than signifying a fundamental hatred of women, Peña argues that these men's public displays of "machismo" should be viewed as a defensive reaction to their own oppressed *class* status:

> As an expression of working-class culture, the folklore of machismo can be considered a realized signifying system [that] points to, but simultaneously displaces, a class relationship and its attendant conflict. At the same time, it introduces a third element, the gender relationship, which acts as a mediator between the signifier (the folklore) and the signified (the class relationship). (p. 40)

In other words, Peña is arguing that undocumented Mexican immigrant men are unable to directly confront their class oppressors, so instead they symbolically displace their class antagonism into the arena of gender relations. Similar arguments have been made about other groups of marginalized and subordinated men. For instance, David Collinson (1988) argues that Australian male blue-collar workers commonly engage in sexually aggressive and misogynist humor in an (ultimately flawed) means of bonding together to resist the control of management males (who are viewed, disparagingly, as feminized). These observations are similar to Majors's (1995) claim that young black males tend to embody and publicly display an expressive and often sexually aggressive style of masculinity that acts as a form of resistance to racism. These studies make important strides toward building an understanding of how subordinated and marginalized groups of men tend to embody and publicly display styles of masculinity that at least symbolically resist the various forms of oppression that they face within hierarchies of intermale dominance.

Yet in foregrounding the oppression of men by men, these studies risk portraying aggressive, even misogynist, gender displays primarily as liberating forms of resistance against class and racial oppression (e.g., Mirandé, 1982). What is obscured or even drops out of sight is the feminist observation that these kinds of masculinity are forms of domination over women. As a result, women's actual experiences of oppression and victimization by men's violence are conspicuously absent from most of these analyses, thus leaving the impression that misogyny is merely a "symbolic displacement" of men's experience of class (or race) subordination. The dangers in this class and race reductionism are most apparent when we recognize that misogyny does not simply reside in the realm of the symbolic; it is also closely tied to what men *do*. Two examples illustrate how class and race reductionists simultaneously can be critical of black males' acts of violence against women and at the same time explain these phenomena largely as a displaced response to racism and, more subtly, as retaliation against black women's power over boys and men. Majors, Tyler, Peden, and Hall (1994), highly critical of domestic violence, explain its prevalence among blacks in the following way:

> Often, male-female conflict develops when a female criticizes a male for his inability or failure to support the family, when she raises her voice at him, or, even worse, when she raises her voice at him around "the guys." Many Black males feel that any of these criticisms are a direct insult to their manhood. Because they feel that such remarks display disloyalty and disrespect, these males often become violent to "save face." Essentially, many Black men feel that, even though they may not be able to control how the white man or society treats them, they at the very least should be able to control their women. (p. 253)

Similarly, Staples (1995b) acknowledges that high rates of rape by young black males result from sexist socialization, but ultimately he sees rape as a "political act" in response to powerlessness:

> [Black males] grow up feeling emasculated and powerless before reaching manhood. They often encounter women as authority figures or as the head of their household. These men consequently act out their feelings of powerlessness against Black women in the form of sexual aggression. Hence, rape by Black men should be viewed as both an aggressive and political act because it occurs in the context of racial discrimination which denies most Black men a satisfying manhood. (p. 378)

Obviously, these arguments are flawed in the ways that they portray the victims of domestic violence and rape—women—as empowered agents and the perpetrators of these acts—black men—as the disempowered victims. On a theoretical level, the source of this blind spot lies in the fact that many radical scholars of race relations are still mired in a simplistic and mechanistic Marxism that sees the economic "base" as the major cause of all other forms of oppression. For instance, Bowser (1994, p. 125) explains the cause of "exaggerated Black male sexuality" with the following sequence:

Economic and social marginality → Frustrated role fulfillment → Marginality as husband/father/manfriend → Compensation in sexuality in male/female relations

Clearly, examination of issues such as domestic violence, exaggerated sexuality, and rape as a distorted compensation for or response to *men's* experience of powerlessness fails to address the experience of the main victims of these behaviors—women. And although there is undoubtedly an important grain of truth to the racial and economic causal argument, this approach does not fully or adequately explain the causes of men's violence against women. After all, domestic violence and rape are also committed by many class-privileged white men who presumably have no experience of racial or class subordination to "compensate" for. What is needed, then, is an examination of masculine gender displays, power, and violence within the context of intersecting systems of class, race, and gender relations (Hondagneu-Sotelo & Messner, 1994). From this point of view, it is more likely that rather than viewing "masculinity" as a desired social role to which men of color have been denied access, theorists and activists will come to "identify the deeper problem—namely, that there is something wrong with the concept of 'masculinity' itself" (Segal, 1990, p. 188). From this critical feminist perspective, it may then become clear that the pursuit of this masculinity—rather than liberating men—tends to lock men into self-destructive behaviors and into oppressive, hierarchical, and destructive relations with women and with other men.

To this day, the dominant discourse in men of color's racial politics has not taken this critical feminist approach. As a result, the dominant forms of political organizing—both in their conservative essentialist and radical reductionist forms—have sought uncritically to strengthen or shore up "black masculinity." For instance, in recent years, in response to the crisis faced by young black males, community leaders and some educators have advocated "manhood training" and/or all-male public schools for young black males. In language that is sometimes similar to that of the leaders of the mythopoetic men's movement, advocates of this strategy assume that there is a desired masculinity to which young black males are being denied access, due to lack of initiation by adult male role models and an overproliferation of adult female influences. Richard Majors (1994), an advocate of schools for young black males (staffed primarily by black males), explains it in this way:

> Black boys are socialized to see females more sexually than are white boys; this socialization creates conflicts when females are in authority roles. Thus, at or around fourth grade (age eight or nine), many young Black boys begin to have trouble with female authority figures. Also, many Black boys come from fatherless homes; they need opportunities to see, touch, and talk to adult Black male role models in order to develop appropriate masculine roles. (p. 310)

The need for adult black males to take responsibility for training and initiating young black males into masculinity was also a key theme in the Million Man March. To be sure, if the March leaders' calls for black men to care more for their own biological children, to adopt 25,000 black children, and to volunteer with organizations such as Big Brothers actually turn into widespread actions, this will be a tremendously positive outcome of the MMM for black children, women, and men alike. On the other hand, the dominant discourse of the MMM, with its conservative views of family and its essentialist and/or reductionist views of "manhood," appears to preclude the building of alliances with progressive feminist women, gay and lesbian organizations, or profeminist men's organizations. Indeed, the fact that the only mention of coalition building in the MMM mission statement called for "building appropriate alliances with other peoples of color" (Karenga, 1995, p. 10) but not with any other progressive groups tends to underline the extent to which this men's movement is narrowly focused on racial identity politics, rather than being more broadly focused on the building of progressive coalitions.

Gay Male Liberation

Sparked by the Stonewall Rebellion but with deeper historical roots, the gay liberation movement took off in the 1970s in the United States. Whereas its predecessor, the homophile movement of the 1940s, 1950s, and early 1960s, had relied on a liberal assimilationist strategy, the gay liberation movement adopted the more radical discourse of the black, youth, and women's liberation movements of the day (Adam, 1977, 1995; Nardi, Sanders, & Marmor, 1994). Carl Wittman's (1970) "Gay Manifesto" reflected this radicalism in its call for "sexual self-determination, the abolition of sex-role stereotypes and the human right to the use of one's own body without interference from legal and social institutions of the state" (p. 93). Also in 1970, a North American coalition of gay liberation organizations (cited in Adam, 1977) came together under the credo, "Don't adjust your mind: Reality has a flaw in it," and demanded

> (1) coalition of the gay movement with the movements of other oppressed peoples, such as blacks, women, Chicanos, and Indians; (2) struggle against social control institutions, such as government, church, business, and medicine; (3) rejection of heterosexist standards of morality and sexual repression; (4) right of self-definition; (5) abolition of age-of-consent laws; (6) opposition to the United States presence in Vietnam. (p. 292)

This broad concern with coalition building, especially the stated goal of linking the fight against heterosexism with the women's movement, placed radical gay men in a unique position with respect to the early growth of men's liberationism, men's profeminism, and profeminist scholarship on men (Nichols, 1977; Williams, 1986). In the heady moments of the early 1970s, it seemed to many that the very existence of a gay subculture could help to undermine one of the key elements of hegemonic masculinity. In the pre-gay liberation era, an unambiguously heterosexual orientation was considered to be a necessary prereq- uisite if a man was to be considered "masculine." By comparison, homosexual men were placed in binary opposition to "normal" (i.e., straight, masculine) men—to be a homosexual man was supposedly synonymous with being defined as "effeminate," as womanlike. The rise of public gay male communities appeared to challenge this simple notion, and this challenge appears ultimately to have given rise to counterattacks in the form of rising levels of antigay violence, per- petrated mostly by young males who identify as "straight" (Herek, 1991).

Yet it also became clear by the mid- to late 1970s that gay liberation was forged in contradiction and paradox (Altman, 1982). As Segal (1990) put it, "however assertively or defensively seeking a space inside the dominant culture, homosexual subcultures have a tantalizing rela- tionship with the masculine ideal—part challenge, part endorsement" (p. 144). It is this simultaneous "challenge and endorsement" of hegemonic masculinity that has led me to place gay liberation in a liminal position in the terrain of the politics of masculinities (see Figure 5.1). The elements of gay liberation that "endorse" hegemonic mascu- linity—focused as they are on liberating individual gay men to enjoy wider lifestyle choices (often including assertive claims to be viewed as "masculine")—tend to pull gay politics toward the lower right "differ- ences between and inequalities among men" corner of the terrain. On the other hand, the elements of gay liberation that challenge hegemonic masculinity—especially the tendency to link gay liberation with femi- nism, lesbian liberation, and other progressive social movements—pull gay liberation closer to the center of the terrain.

In the remainder of this chapter, I will focus on the three related themes in the gay liberation movement that explain its liminal role in the larger politics of masculinities: (a) gay liberation's paradoxical relationship with hegemonic masculinity, (b) gay liberation's tendency to reduce "liberation" to the sexual liberation of men, and (c) gay liberation's tendency to falsely universalize "gay men" and thus to marginalize gay men of color, effeminate men, and poor or working- class men. Combined, these three tendencies have distanced gay libera- tion from its earlier focus on the building of coalitions to bring about radical, institutional changes. Instead, gay liberation has come largely to define itself in the liberal language of individual equal rights and assimilation into a commercial, capitalist order. And rather than chal- lenging or undermining hegemonic masculinity, this assimilationist

tendency in gay liberation has attempted instead to broaden the definition of hegemonic masculinity to include same-sex sexual relations.

Gay Liberation's Paradoxical
Relationship to Masculinity

By the mid- to late 1970s, much of the radical impulse in gay
liberation had already been eclipsed by a more pragmatic, liberal approach that focused on individual rights and lifestyle alternatives. To
be sure, the loss of gay liberation's radical edge reflected what was
happening to other radical and liberation movements of the 1960s and
1970s. And it also reflected a pragmatic move by gay and lesbian leaders
to respond to a dangerous antigay and lesbian attack by the religious
right in the late 1970s. Increasingly, gay and lesbian leaders responded
to this crisis by positioning themselves as "normal people"—endorsing
"family values," private consensual sex, and conventional gender roles
(albeit expanded to include same-sex sexual relations). "We are no
threat," they seemed to be saying to the nation. "We are just like you."

This attempt to normalize or mainstream gay men and lesbians in
terms of dominant conceptions of gender was more than a defensive
strategy. It also reflected a growing impulse within gay male communities to embrace hegemonic masculinity. In 1977, Jack Nichols, who had
been working for several years to establish links between the gay
liberation and men's liberation movements, noted that gay men have a
unique understanding of "the facades of what passes for masculinity in
our culture" (p. 328). Because gay men were often well aware of having
put on "masks" of masculinity, they were in a unique position to
illuminate the fact that masculinity is a social construction rather than
a fact of nature. However, Nichols lamented, gay culture seemed to be
developing a love affair with hypermasculine displays of emotional and
physical hardness and simultaneously devaluing anything considered
feminine. By the late 1970s, this "butch shift" in gay communities was
clearly the dominant trend (Altman, 1982). There even seemed to be a
fascinating reversal of the previously taken-for-granted relationship
between sexual orientation and gender displays, as "gay men could be
distinguished by their *more* masculine appearance. Meanwhile many
heterosexual men were displaying a perfumed, fashion-conscious,
more narcissistic and androgynous masculinity" (Segal, 1990, p. 149).

The high value placed on displays of hegemonic masculinity in gay
communities is not that difficult to explain. After all, gay men have been
taught that masculinity is valued and rewarded in the culture but

femininity is devalued and subordinated. "Men," Nichols (1977) noted, "whether gay or straight identified, are taught to cling to masculinism (without any clear idea of what it is) with greater urgency than they are taught anything else" (p. 329). It shouldn't be too surprising that many gay men—having experienced the imposition of a socially devalued and despised "effeminate" gay male stereotype—increasingly came to define gay male liberation *not* in opposition to hegemonic masculinity but, rather, as a claim to be "just as masculine as the next guy" (Nichols, 1977, p. 330).

Gay men's claims to the rights and status of manhood were similar, in some ways, to the claims that were being made at roughly the same time by male black power advocates. Having been denied full masculine status, rights, and privileges, these marginalized and subordinated groups of men were now attempting to seize and publicly display the dominant cultural symbols of manhood. For gay men, this was perhaps best symbolized by the explosion in the popularity of bodybuilding (Klein, 1993). And as more gay men continued to "come out" of the closets in the late 1970s, these included men such as professional football player David Kopay (Kopay & Young, 1977) and Olympic decathlete Tom Waddell (Messner, 1994), both of whom saw their participation in competitive and aggressive sports as a way to stake claims to manhood and to disrupt the culture's equation of gayness with femininity. Meanwhile, the newly hegemonic hard and tough gay masculinity was serving to marginalize and subordinate effeminate gay men within gay communities. In response to the emergence of an eroticized gender hierarchy within gay male communities, a group of radical men in 1973 penned "The Effeminist Manifesto," which indicted gay liberation for being one of the "male ideologies" through which gay men had become "collaborators with patriarchy" (Dansky, Knoebel, & Pitchford, 1977, p. 116). In short, despite the potential of gay liberation to strip off the masks of masculinity, it appears that the dominant tendency in gay culture eventually became an attempt to claim, eroticize, and display the dominant symbols of hegemonic masculinity.

Gay Liberation as Sexual Liberation

The growth of "gay ghettos," gay communities, and gay liberation did not arise primarily as a response to gender oppression but to the *sexual* oppression of men who had sex (or wanted to have sex) with other men. To be sure, from the very beginning, there were tentative but important links between gay male and lesbian liberation movements.

But in the gay and lesbian liberation movement, lesbians tended to be underrepresented, especially in leadership positions. And importantly, from the outset of the movement, lesbians had increasingly tended to identify as feminists, leading many of them to identify at least as much with the gender claims made by women's liberation groups as with the sexual claims being made by gay liberation groups (Echols, 1989; Esterberg, 1994). Whereas this had the effect of pulling some gay men into profeminist discourse and activism in the 1970s and beyond, most gay male liberationists appear to have defined "liberation" primarily in terms of their own *sexual* liberation.

This tension between gay male liberationists and feminists is most apparent in the continuing debates about pornography that peaked in the mid-1980s. Feminists (especially radical feminists, as I outlined in Chapter 4) tended to view pornography *in terms of gender relations*, as the key link in men's sexual objectification and bodily oppression of women. Gay liberationists tended to view pornography *in terms of sexual liberation*. In the context of a heterosexist society that told them that their own feelings and desires were sick and/or sinful, many gay men had experienced pornography as their first positive affirmation of same-sex sexual desire and pleasure. In short, pornography was a key link in the liberation process for many gay men. The stakes appeared high for both groups: Radical feminists saw pornography as "violence against women," and gay male liberationists believed that efforts to ban or limit pornography—by feminists or by the religious right—represented threats to their very identities and communities. As feminist antipornography groups, such as Women Against Pornography (WAP), conducted "guided tours" of pornography districts in major cities with the aim of illuminating and disrupting sexual violence against women, many gay men acted affirmatively to defend gay pornography (e.g., Clark, 1990; Tucker, 1990; Weinstein, 1990).

Through the late 1980s, most profeminist men chose to adopt radical feminist women's gender focus rather than gay men's sexual focus on the issue of pornography. This led some gay men to argue strongly against the "privileging of gender" in profeminist male scholarship and activism. In a challenge to heterosexual "men's studies" scholars to "counter the damaging effects of some feminist analyses . . . of pornography, misogyny, intergenerational sex, and liberationist perspectives on sex," Dowsett (1993) argues that, in the work of such scholars, too often gay male representations of gay men's bodies and their imaging of gay men's desire are read with women's eyes. The "passive" anus is read as an analogue to the "dominated" vagina. . . . Gay men's readings of these images is deemed secondary to a feminist reading, and the definitions of issues, bodies, and meanings related to the problems of heterosexuality are privileged over those relating to gay men's sexuality. (pp. 700-701)

Others, such as John D'Emilio (1992), attempted to build bridges of understanding between gay views that emphasized sexual liberation and feminist views that emphasized how male sexuality is shaped to perpetuate violence and oppression of women:

My response to WAP and to pornography was shaped by my experience as a gay man. Both terms are significant. As someone gay, I knew that gay life often took place in pornographic zones, making that space precious for me. As a man, I also knew that in our culture the meaning and significance of pornography are deeply gendered: porn simply doesn't carry for me the aura of danger that it does for many women. That fact is both virtue and defect. It allows me to view pornography from a different vantage point even as it might obscure other angles of vision. (p. 202)

In 1990, Michael Kimmel brought together a valuable collection of essays titled *Men Confront Pornography* that provided a forum for dialogue among gay liberationists, antipornography profeminists, and others. More recently, some gay men of color have begun to further broaden this discussion. For example, Richard Fung's (1996) essay transcends—and potentially bridges—the seemingly irreconcilable positions taken by radical feminists and most gay male liberationists on the pornography debate. Fung argues that for Asian American gay men, gay pornography and the mainstream gay movement

can be a place of freedom and sexual identity. But it is also a site of racial, cultural, *and* sexual alienation sometimes more pronounced than in straight society. For me sex is a source of pleasure, but also a site of humiliation and pain. . . . Porn can be an active agent in representing *and* reproducing a sex-race status quo. (pp. 191-192)

Because he experiences both the liberating and oppressive realities of pornography, Fung cannot endorse a purely "libertarian" approach to pornography, as many mainstream gay male liberationists have, but neither does he endorse the radical feminist position that favors the eradication of pornography. Rather, he cautiously urges the creation of "an independent gay Asian pornography," in much the same way that some feminists have urged the development of an erotica produced by and for women.

Though significant and important, these sorts of bridges between feminist and gay male positions on pornography are quite limited in scope. Just as the dominant discourse and practice in racialized politics of masculinity are to reduce the liberation of men of color to a struggle against racial oppression, so too the dominant discourse and practice of gay liberationists have been to reduce the liberation of gay men to sexual liberation. And in both cases, embodiments and displays of hegemonic masculinity are seen as a means to this liberation.

The False Universalization of "Gay Men"

As gay men and lesbians began to come out in great numbers in the early and mid-1970s, the belief in a uniquely "gay experience" and "gay identity" was a key element in the forging of "the gay community" (Weston, 1991). The notion that all gay men and lesbians could share their "coming-out stories" created a sense of a shared experience of oppression and commitment to liberation (Plummer, 1995). This sense of community was a key factor in uniting gay men and lesbians to fight against attempts by the religious right to roll back gay and lesbian rights in the late 1970s and 1980s, and it has continued to provide an important basis in the 1980s and 1990s for organizing against the AIDS epidemic.

However, the belief that "we are family" in "the gay community" also served to veil the often oppressive inequalities that existed *within* this community. The movement's leaders and spokespeople were mainly white, more often than not men, college-educated, and of the professional class. Moreover, as Soares pointed out in 1979, "racism in the gay subculture is a reality that all black gay people deal with" (p. 263). More recently, Peterson (1992) noted that men who identify as black and gay often develop "dual identities in conflict, as they attempt to negotiate, and often are forced to choose, between two communities, neither of which fully accepts them" (p. 150). If they choose to identify primarily as gay (rather than as black), Peterson notes, they often face overt and covert racial discrimination and prejudice in white-dominated gay communities. Similarly, Chicano and Latino gay men are often marginalized in gay communities (Almaguer, 1991; Carrier, 1992).

The fiction of the gay community also tended to veil the existence of huge economic inequities—between gay men and lesbians, between older and younger gay men, and between white gay men and gay men of color. Since the 1970s, a large part of the stabilization of gay communities, as well as the basis of the relative power of gay politics in many cities, has involved the growth of "gay capitalism." But as Dennis Altman (1982) argues, the growth of gay capitalism also has resulted in a "commercialization of desire," which has served to undercut the earlier radical impulses of gay liberation:

> It is ironic that as we have become freer in our sexuality we seem to have become more reliant on business institutions to provide us with the means to express this freedom. . . . Much so-called sexual liberation has not, by and large, made for a genuine eroticism of everyday life as much as it has meant the creation of a set of specialized institutions within which people can, for a certain time that is quite consciously divorced from their everyday lives, act out sexual fantasies. (p. 85)

In short, the idea that there is *a* gay male experience that has formed the basis of *the* gay community was a key to the development of a successful and empowering gay politics of identity. But this normalized gay identity was based on a falsely universalized white, upper-middle-class, and highly masculine gay male experience, thus tending to render invisible the experience of lesbians, gay men of color, poor and working-class gay men, and effeminate gay men. By the late 1970s, radical critics bemoaned the fact that gay liberation had been co-opted by capitalism and by the "born-again politics of respectability" through which gay men had become "willing to embrace the assimilationist formula, adopting symbols of conformity in return for (often vicarious) participation in the privileges of their class and sex" (Adam, 1977, pp. 296-297). "The single greatest disillusionment of the last few years," Michael Silverstein (1977) wrote, "is being forced to admit that the revolutionary potential of gay men just isn't true. . . . Many gay men, maybe most, just want their piece of the pie, and if they're already doing pretty well in terms of class and race, then gayness doesn't seem that big a barrier" (p. 194).

In retrospect, we should temper these late 1970s claims of "disillusionment" with gay liberation's "revolutionary potential." After all, the other progressive social movements of the 1960s and early 1970s had by then either completely fallen apart or had shifted into a more liberal discourse of individualism and equal rights. And some of the more radical elements of gay liberation still continued to influence the profeminist men's movement and, more recently, the emergent "queer" movements among youth. Dowsett (1993) responds to the charge that gay men have been co-opted into middle-class respectability by defiantly arguing that "the attempt to make gay men sexually respectable is being resisted and will be resisted to the last orgasm" (p. 704). And Connell (1995) argues that despite most gay men's conservative affirmations of masculinity and despite their tendency to reduce "liberation" to calls for individual rights to pursue their own sexual choices, the very existence of "homosexual masculinity" is a destabilizing "subversion" in patriarchal society (pp. 161-162).

Movements by racially or sexually marginalized and subordinated groups of men are sociologically fascinating for the very reason that they so consistently express such a contradictory and paradoxical relationship to "masculinity." To the extent that men of color or gay men stake claims to masculinity as a means of fighting racism or heterosexism, the outcome of their political organizing is likely to be beneficial in some limited ways to some of these men. But their potential for engaging in progressive coalition politics that is capable of confronting the structured system of social inequalities that oppresses them is quite limited. On the other hand, to the extent that these groups begin to see through, criticize, and work to change conventional definitions of masculinity, they represent a tremendous potential for the development of coalition politics in the coming decades. One theme in the final chapter will explore how gay men of color, in particular, can (and sometimes do) provide "bridges" that link groups in a politics of progressive coalition building.

Notes

1. The National Park Service's initial crowd count of 400,000 was immediately protested and contested by the organizers of the MMM. Psychologist A. J. Franklin (cited in Boyd, 1995) said that the undercount was an example of "deep denial. This is merely another attempt to keep us invisible" (p. 12). By contrast, experts from Boston University estimated the crowd at 837,000, with a margin of error of 20%.

2. A Howard University survey of the marchers found that 41% reported that their annual incomes were above $50,000, and 77% reported annual incomes above $25,000, placing most of them well above the $18,500 median annual income for black males (Boyd, 1995).

CHAPTER 6

Backlash or Social Justice?

Make no mistake about it: Women want a men's movement. We are literally dying for it. If you doubt that, just listen to women's desperate testimonies of hope that the men in our lives will become more nurturing toward children, more able to talk about emotions, less hooked on a spectrum of control that extends from not listening through to violence, and less repressive of their own human qualities that are called "feminine."

—*Gloria Steinem (1992, p. v)*

The structural problem of counter-sexist politics among men needs to be stated plainly, as it is constantly evaded. The familiar forms of radical politics rely on mobilizing solidarity around a shared interest. That is common to working-class politics, national liberation movements, feminism, and gay liberation. This *cannot* be the main form of counter-sexist politics among men, because the project of social justice in gender relations is directed *against* the interests they share. Broadly speaking, anti-sexist politics must be a source of disunity among men, not a source of solidarity. There is a rigorous logic to the trends of the 1980's: The more men's groups and their gurus emphasized solidarity among men (being "positive about men," seeking the "deep masculine," etc.), the more willing they became to abandon issues of social justice.

—*R. W. Connell (1995, p. 236)*

In this final chapter, I will move beyond locating and analyzing individual men's movements, as I have done throughout most of this book. Instead, I will push the analytic utility of the terrain of the politics of masculinities model a bit further. First, I will discuss the implications of a movement's being located in certain geographical sites within this political terrain. Concurrently, I will discuss existing, emergent, or potential alliances or conflicts between groups or between fragments of groups. In other words, I would like to suggest here that, rather than simply staking out and occupying a fixed position within the terrain of the politics of masculinities, there is considerable dynamism and movement operating here. The actual (or potential) dynamism and movement is grounded in (a) internal fissures, contradictions, and disagreements *within* seemingly coherent and stable groups and (b) dialogue, conflict, and/or cooperation *among* different groups over specific political issues. Next, I will critically assess the extent to which the current antisexist men's movement, as represented mainly by NOMAS in the United States, is a potential nexus for the development of progressive alliances among those who are working for social justice. Finally, I will suggest that recent ideas developed mostly by feminist women of color, such as the notion of "multiracial feminism," might offer the best point of departure for a progressive politics.

Contemporary Terrains of Gender Politics

In Figure 6.1, I have divided the by now familiar conceptual terrain of the politics of masculinities into four sections. A group's location within this terrain has implications for the role(s) it plays or can play in current gender (and race, class, and/or sexuality) politics. Thus far, I have been concerned mainly with what goes on "inside" the triad—that is, I have focused on groups that overtly see themselves and organize themselves in terms of "men's issues" or "masculinity issues." But in each of these cases, an overtly self-conscious politics of masculinities is only a part of a larger political terrain, and to reflect this, I have drawn circles around the three corners of the triad that extend beyond its borders.

The Terrain of Antifeminist Backlash

As Figure 6.1 illustrates, the lower left corner of the triad is part of a larger terrain of antifeminist (and usually also antigay and antilesbian) backlash. Near the center of the terrain of antifeminist backlash is Promise Keepers, whose phenomenal recent growth and overtly antifeminist and antigay political agenda puts them at the cutting edge of a large, though itself internally fragmented, "religious right" movement. As I discussed in Chapter 2, this conservative impulse in masculinity politics has its recent roots in the "moral majority" and other antifeminist, antigay, antiabortion, and antipornography organizations that positioned themselves as "profamily" in the 1970s and 1980s (Lienesch, 1990). The dramatic emergence of Promise Keepers illustrates a new stage in this larger movement, a stage in which a massive group

FIGURE 6.1

The Terrain of the Politics of Masculinities: The Current State of Play Between and Among Various Movements

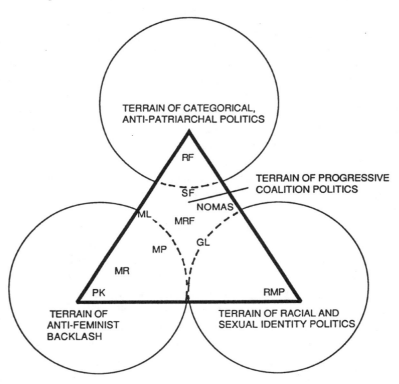

TERRAIN OF CATEGORICAL,
ANTI-PATRIARCHAL POLITICS

RF

TERRAIN OF PROGRESSIVE
COALITION POLITICS

SF

NOMAS

ML

MRF

MP

GL

MR

PK

RMP

TERRAIN OF
ANTI-FEMINIST
BACKLASH

TERRAIN OF RACIAL AND
SEXUAL IDENTITY POLITICS

PK = Promise Keepers
MP = Mythopoetic Men's Movement
ML = Men's Liberation Movement
MR = Men's Rights Movement
RF = Radical Feminist Men
SF = Socialist Feminist Men

GL = Gay Liberation Movement
RMP = Racialized Masculinity Politics
MRF = Multiracial Feminism
NOMAS = National Organization for
       Men Against Sexism

of men is self-consciously asserting that it is the their group's responsibility—*as men*—to take the leadership role.

To what extent is Promise Keepers concerned with other "men's movements"? Clearly, some of the more therapeutically oriented ideas and values from the "men's liberation" and "human potential" movements of the 1970s and 1980s inform Promise Keepers' discourse, especially in its focus on stopping men's self-destructive practices, such as alcohol and drug abuse. By 1996, there was considerable evidence that the mostly white Promise Keepers was beginning to reach out to African American and other Christian men of color. In the wake of the Million Man March, Promise Keepers' leaders appear to have seen the remarkable similarity between their own values and goals and those of many who organized the MMM. In short, both groups are spiritually based movements that are calling on men to stop their self-destructiveness, stop their violence, and bond together with other men to retake responsibility for caring for and leading their families, their communities, and their nation. Although Promise Keepers might see this affinity with Million Man Marchers as an opportunity to expand its base, its main frame of reference in terms of their organizational and political identity is clearly not other "men's movements." Rather, Promise Keepers defines itself primarily in relation to the larger conservative movement that lies mostly "outside" the terrain that I have been concerned with mapping out in this book. Promise Keepers might see fit to attempt to recruit from other men's organizations, but it is very unlikely that they will ever consider exploring alliances with other groups within the terrain of the politics of masculinities that I have mapped out.

A bit further from the center of the terrain of antifeminist backlash is the men's rights movement. As I pointed out in Chapter 3, men's rights advocates are similar to Promise Keepers in their belief that feminists have caused many of the problems that men and contemporary families face. And both groups argue that men need to be reempowered, as men. But beyond these general similarities, Promise Keepers and the men's rights movement differ dramatically. Whereas Promise Keepers has essentialist beliefs in "traditional male-female roles," which are based fundamentally on naturalized conceptions of men's position as family leaders, most men's rights advocates are social constructionists who believe that masculinity needs to be reconstructed in more egalitarian and peaceful directions. What's more, although their constituency is predominantly heterosexual fathers, men's rights groups are not overtly antigay as is Promise Keepers. Yet their "men's rights" discourse and practice—sometimes taken to the extreme of outright misogyny—situate men's rights activists firmly within the terrain of antifeminist politics.

Though their "fathers' rights" focus is more limited in scope than Promise Keepers' far-ranging broadside attack on the whole concept of equality, if the men's rights movement is successful in achieving its organizational goals, the results would clearly move us away from, rather than toward, equality between women and men. However, their differences from Promise Keepers illustrate the fact that within the terrain of antifeminist backlash, there are fissures, differences, even potential conflicts. For instance, I would speculate that it is highly unlikely that we will see any direct alliances between these two groups. Though they may share a disdain for feminism, men's rights activists are unlikely to agree with most of the antigay, prohierarchy, and pro "traditional family" views of Promise Keepers. Similarly, Promise Keepers is very unlikely to agree with the men's rights' social constructionist view that argues for a reconstruction of social life so that fathers have full rights to care for and nurture children. In fact, underlying Promise Keepers' beliefs is an essentialist defense of mothers' and fathers' natural roles as, respectively, female nurturers and male leaders and breadwinners.

Finally, I locate the mythopoetic men's movement at the outer edge of the terrain of antifeminist backlash and on the doorstep (but not inside) of the terrain of progressive coalition building. In Chapter 2, I discussed the backlash potential of mythopoetic discourse—especially its valorization of an essentialized inner "warrior masculinity," its emphasis on men's pain, and its silence about white, professional-class men's positions in a system of inequality that oppresses women and some groups of men. Clearly, this focus on men's pain—and the barely submerged suggestion that women, especially feminists, might be responsible for much of this pain—creates a psychological and organization potential for antifeminist politics (Hagan, 1992). Indeed, there is some evidence that the outcome of "men's work" for at least some mythopoetic men has been the creation of a homosocial space in which to express anger and blame toward women (Schwalbe, 1996). Once in this space, it is easy to speculate that those mythopoetic men who do have an interest in participating in overt gender politics (as opposed to individual spiritual growth or therapy) might find themselves attracted to the men's rights movement. A recent book edited by Michael Kimmel (1995b) provides some concrete examples of this mythopoetic and men's rights confluence. At the end of the book, which consists mostly of essays by profeminist men who are criticizing the mythopoetic men's movement, several mythopoetic leaders respond. Two of them, Marvin Allen (1995) and Aaron Kipnis (1995), scolded their profeminist critics for ignoring the "credible" ideas of "postfeminist social commentators" such as men's rights leaders Herb Goldberg, Asa Barber, and Warren Farrell. In other words, some mythopoetic leaders clearly feel an affinity with men's rights beliefs and feel that the criticisms of their movement by feminists are "vituperative, twisted, and insidiously conspiratorial" (Kipnis, 1995, p. 278).

On the other hand, many men in the mythopoetic movement, including Robert Bly himself, consider themselves to be "progressive" and "left-liberals" (Bly, 1995; Schwalbe, 1996). Though they tend to define mythopoetic "men's work" as apolitical, there have been a number of grassroots mythopoetic men who simultaneously have been involved in profeminist men's organizations, such as NOMAS, for a number of years. For these men, the spiritual bonding and healing that they find in the mythopoetic movement complements the profeminist and gay affirmative political activities of NOMAS (Dash, 1995; Schwalbe, 1995b). In fact, some members of the mythopoetic men's movement have argued that there has always been a profeminist impulse within their organization. These more politically progressive elements in the mythopoetic movement have been ignored due to the media's and to profeminists' simplistic assumption that the writings of Robert Bly express the ideas of the entire movement. Instead, they point out, leaders such as Michael Meade, James Hillman, and Sam Keen have argued that progressive engagement with feminist political action is an important dimension of mythopoetic men's work (see Blauner, 1996; Bliss, 1995). Reflecting this tendency in the movement and the existing bridge building at the grass roots of these organizations, some mythopoetic and profeminist leaders have recently declared a need to move beyond confrontation and "defining turf" toward productive dialogue. For instance, Robert Bly recently has begun a personal dialogue with Michael Kimmel of the National Organization of Men Against Sexism (NOMAS), and Bly was invited to address the 1996 NOMAS meeting, while Kimmel was invited to address a 1996 mythopoetic meeting (see Bly, 1995; Kimmel, 1995a). The need for such dialogue has seemed increasingly urgent to leaders in both movements, especially in light of the growth of reactionary movements such as Promise Keepers.

Though some mythopoetic men may be attracted closer to the heart of antifeminist backlash terrain and some may be attracted to progressive coalition building, it is likely that for the foreseeable future most mythopoetic discourse and practice will remain overtly apolitical. But the "apolitical" still has political consequences. Clearly, the mythopoetic men's movement is not at the angry and mean-spirited heart of antifeminist backlash. But when members of a relatively privileged group organize themselves around a shared identity that is shaped by that privilege, and they refuse to recognize or confront that privilege, then they are covertly supporting the system that privileges them.

The Terrain of Categorical Antipatriarchal Politics

Men's contributions to radical, antipatriarchal politics in the United States have been minimal, to say the least. This relatively low level of discourse and activity by men within radical feminist politics is reflected in Figure 6.1, where the circle that represents antipatriarchal politics includes only a small portion of the upper corner of the triad of masculinity politics. But to the extent that they have been actively involved, a relatively small network of radical feminist men has had an impressive impact. As I discussed in Chapter 4, radical feminist discourse tends toward categorical views of women and men as, respectively, oppressed and oppressor sex classes. These categorical views are often grounded in a nearly exclusive focus on bodily oppressions, with sexuality being seen as the major nexus of men's bodily oppression of women. The view that bodies—and particularly, sexual bodies—are the locus of patriarchal oppression provides radical feminist politics with a singular focus for antipatriarchal actions. Moreover, the focus on extremes of bodily abuse, violence, and oppression (such as rape, violent pornography, wife beating, etc.) provides a powerfully emotional moral basis and impetus for action. Thus, a relatively small number of radical feminist men have been moved to focus their energies on antirape, antipornography, and anti-wife-beating education and counseling, in addition to supporting feminist efforts to change or enact laws that aim to empower women to avoid and resist men's violence. In short, given their small numbers, radical feminist men have had a disproportionately large impact in the communities in which they work. And given the often singular moral basis from which they work, their discourse has had a powerful impact on debates within the larger antisexist men's movement.

Radical feminist politics of masculinity has its limits, though. First, its categorical focus on men tends to falsely universalize men's experiences. This categoricalism obliterates an understanding of how other systems of inequality, such as social class, race, and sexuality intersect with gender in ways that limit and constrain marginalized and subordinated groups of men's ability to "cash in" on the "patriarchal dividend" (Connell, 1995). Second, the radical feminist focus on "male sexuality" as an embodiment of power and "female sexuality" as an embodiment of women's subordination borders on an essentialist view of gender difference that undercuts social constructionist views of gender and sexuality. At its extreme, this view tends to present male sexuality as some essential will among men to eroticize violence and domination of women (Segal, 1987). To renounce it appears to be to renounce sexual pleasure altogether. Indeed, it is interesting to read radical feminist John Stoltenberg's (1995) description and analysis of the Promise Keepers' mass meeting that he attended. Though he is very critical of Promise Keepers for its antifeminist views, he confesses to having gained a grudging respect for them by meeting's end:

> To a man, they seem more polite, pleasant, and personable than I have ever encountered among large numbers of other men in public space. Their shared sense of decency in everyday ethics is not to be sneered at (I know of no secular equivalent any better, no movement of "men of conscience" anywhere leftward politically). (p. 52)

And the "decency in everyday ethics" among Promise Keepers that seems to impress Stoltenberg the most lies in its renunciation of sex-for-pleasure. Stoltenberg's appreciation of Promise Keepers' antisexuality position stands in stark contrast to his scathing indictment, discussed in Chapter 4, of gay male liberationist "propornography" activists, whom he views as supporting a social context that creates violence against women. In fact, Stoltenberg goes so far as to suggest that Promise Keepers' strong antipornography stance cannot be simply written off as "anti-smut" but demonstrates that "religious conservatives have actually been paying quite close attention to radical feminism, and learning a lot" (p. 26). I would argue, rather, that the confluence between Stoltenberg's and Promise Keepers' positions on sexuality and pornography echoes the uneasy and troubled "alliance" in the 1980s between antipornography radical feminists with the moral majority and religious right. Though opposing pornography for somewhat different reasons, the antipornography feminists and the antipornography conservatives share a view of sexuality as a realm of danger rather than (or even, rather than in addition to) a realm of pleasure (Segal, 1994). And both tend to hold neo-Victorian assumptions, that at the heart of male sexuality there is an *essentially* aggressive, violent, and dominating impulse that must be renounced for the good of civilization. I make this point about Stoltenberg's grudging respect for Promise

Keepers not to suggest the possibility of an alliance emerging between the two—this is nearly impossible to imagine, given their almost diametrically opposed views on most issues related to gender. But I do make the point to illustrate how the categorical, essentialist, and moralistic views of radical feminist men are, in a way, the flip side of those of Promise Keepers. These kinds of views make it very unlikely that radical feminist men will ever be in the forefront of forging progressive alliances with other groups such as gay men and feminist women and men of color.

The Terrain of Racial and Sexual Identity Politics

As Figure 6.1 illustrates, I have placed "Racialized Masculinity Politics" near the lower right corner of the triad and at the center of the "terrain of racial and sexual identity politics." Though it has become a very popular way to describe people who do not identify as "white," the category "people of color" is multifaceted, internally fissured, and complex. Clearly, there are important cultural, language, ethnic, geographical, religious, sexual, and class variations among "men of color" that differentiate their experiences, views, and potential political alliances in ways that make it difficult—even dangerous—to speak of them as a coherent group. Indeed, it is likely that the only thing that makes "men of color" a distinct group is the central role they play as racialized "other" in the social construction of "white masculinity" (Frankenberg, 1993). On the other hand, as I argued in Chapter 5, there are some tentative generalizations that can be drawn about the dominant gender discourse of racialized masculinity politics. In political organizations, as well as in academia, men of color have usually confronted the myriad problems faced by African American, Latino, and Asian American men within analytical frameworks that foreground the causal primacy of racial oppression (sometimes along with class oppression). Overt discussions of masculinity have sometimes emerged within these discourses and practices, but manhood has most often been viewed as an idealized essence or as a social role to which men of color have been denied access by racist and classist institutions. Even men of color who have been critical of sexism have tended to view sexist attitudes and actions toward women as men of color's displaced and distorted reactions to racial and class oppression by other men. As a result, "women's issues" are, at best, relegated to the back burner to await the resolution of the more fundamentally important race and class issues.

To the extent that some leaders among men of color are beginning to place issues of "black manhood" at the center of their discourse and practices (e.g., Louis Farrakhan, as discussed in Chapter 5), it is often a discourse of gender that is at the service of a larger discourse of race and class issues. Thus, it is unlikely that this sort of conservative strand of "manhood discourse" within Afrocentric or other racial discourses will ever link up with any of the politics of masculinities that I have discussed in this book. It is possible, of course, that some Christian African American men might respond to Promise Keepers' reaching out to them. And it is also possible that some conservative Afrocentric men might find it expedient to form tentative alliances with men's rights organizations. For instance, the Afrocentric push for all-male schools for black male children might very well resonate within an emergent men's rights concern with the need to articulate "boys' issues" in school curricula.

In a way, the political discourse and practice of gay liberationists are even more difficult to position accurately in the overall terrain of the politics of masculinities. Despite attempts to define a uniquely "gay community," there is an enormous amount of diversity and inequality among men who identify as gay. As with men of color, the main factor that may give gay men coherence as a social group is the way that they serve to define "heterosexual men" as "normal" (J. N. Katz, 1995). And as I discussed in Chapter 5, gay men as a group have a paradoxical relationship with dominant cultural definitions of masculinity. Their simultaneous "challenge and endorsement" of hegemonic masculinity led me to place gay liberation in a liminal position in the terrain of the politics of masculinities. The elements of gay liberation that endorse hegemonic masculinity—focused as they are on liberating individual gay men to enjoy wider lifestyle choices, celebrating men's muscularity, and generally eroticizing masculine power—tend to pull gay politics toward the lower right corner of the terrain that in previous chapters has been discussed as the "differences and inequalities among men" territory. On the other hand, the elements of gay liberation that challenge hegemonic masculinity—especially the tendency to link gay liberation with feminism, lesbian liberation, and other progressive social movements—pull gay liberation closer to the center of the terrain. In short, as you can see in Figure 6.1, I place gay liberation directly in the space between the more conservative terrain of racial and sexual identity politics and the more radical terrain of progressive coalition politics.

Characteristics of Discourses That
Occupy the Corners of the Terrain

Thus far, I have illustrated that there are particular implications attached to a group's "location" in or near one of the corners of the terrain of the politics of masculinities. Despite the obvious differences in the particular discourses and practices of, for instance, Promise Keepers (in the antifeminist backlash terrain), radical feminist men (in the antipatriarchal politics terrain), and men of color (in the racial identity politics terrain), I would like to point to some general similarities between groups that occupy the corners of the terrain. First, the closer a group's worldview is to a corner of the triad, the more clear-cut and less complicated are their claims about the nature of power, subordination, and oppression. In most cases, this sense of clarity in the political discourse forms a very solid ideological basis for the collective construction of an identity politics for people who share certain experiences or positions in the social structure (e.g., divorced fathers, Christian men, black men, or even, simply, men). This analytical simplicity, along with the sense of clarity and solidarity about who "we" are, can translate—and often has translated—into clearly articulated political (and/or therapeutic) programs. The political projects that emerge from these programs are rarely progressive. The more a group expresses a "costs of masculinity" focus, the more its practices tend to express an antifeminist (and often antigay) backlash that is clearly antithetical to movements for equality and social justice. Groups such as African American men who have emphasized "differences and inequalities among men" have raised and confronted pivotal issues that face men of color, but their lack of a critique of hegemonic masculinity leads to a political stance that, at best, puts "women's issues" in a secondary position to "race and class issues"—at worst, it feeds a single-issue identity politics that pits, for instance, the interests of nonfeminist African American men against those of feminist women. And finally, those who focus almost entirely on men's institutional power and privileges are located in a terrain that encourages morally charged antipatriarchal activism that, though progressive and effective in a limited way, tends to preclude the building of alliances with other progressive groups that do not share the commitment to the idea that male sexual violence is fundamentally at the heart of nearly all forms of oppression.

The Terrain of Progressive Coalition Building

The interior region of the triad that I have labeled "the terrain of progressive coalition politics" is the political territory occupied by groups who attempt to strike some balance between acknowledging men's structural power and privilege, the costs of masculinity, and the race, class, and gender inequalities among men (and among women). The closer a group's worldview is to the center of the triad, the more complex—even contradictory—its internal debates about the social structure of power, inequality, and oppression are likely to be. As a result, these groups have a far more difficult task developing coherent and focused strategies for action.

But it is also true that occupying terrain that is closer to the center of the triad positions a group in a location that maximizes the potential for forging creative coalition building aimed at progressive social change. Discourses and practices that move about this part of the terrain offer the greatest promise for the development of a politics that can simultaneously confront men's structured power and privileges over women (a contribution of radical and socialist profeminist men's movements), in addition to confronting some men's structured power and privileges over subordinated and marginalized groups of men (a contribution of some expressions of racialized masculinity politics, socialist feminism, and gay liberation). It is also within this terrain that this commitment to confronting the privileges of hegemonic masculinity can be joined with the call for a healthy humanization of men that will eliminate the costs of masculinity to men (a contribution made by the progressive wing of the mythopoetic men's movement).

What are the current groups and political discourses that might serve as a nexus for such progressive coalition building as we approach and begin the 21st century? Is the model of a "men's movement" adequate to provide such a nexus? Though I think that profeminist men's organizations can play a key role, I think this role is limited, for various reasons. As the opening paragraph of the "NOMAS Statement of Principles" (NOMAS, 1995) demonstrates, the National Organization for Men Against Sexism has tried to position itself as such a nexus in the United States for roughly two decades:

> The National Organization for Men Against Sexism is an activist or-
> ganization of men and women supporting positive changes for men.
> NOMAS advocates a perspective that is pro-feminist, gay-affirmative,
> and committed to justice on a broad range of social issues including

race, class, age, religion, and physical abilities. We affirm that working to make this nation's ideals of equality substantive is the finest expression of what it means to be men. (p. 529)

The organization, NOMAS, which began as a self-consciously "profeminist, gay-affirmative" organization in the 1970s, has always been committed to creating equality and justice between women and men. For NOMAS, this has meant struggling with women to change the social structure of power (including but not limited to ending men's sexual violence against women) and humanizing men so that they might live happier, healthier lives. This idea of the need to humanize men has always been infused with a critique of the damage that institutionalized heterosexism does to gay men, as well as the ways that homophobia hurts and limits nongay men. Indeed, from its beginnings, NOMAS has been a rare example of an organization in which gay, bisexual, and heterosexually identified men have worked together toward common goals (it is estimated that about half of NOMAS's membership identifies as gay or bisexual).

Through most of the 1980s, though, NOMAS remained an organization that was made up of predominantly white, professional-class men (and some women). Although the organization "welcomed and sought Black men's participation . . . over the years, few blacks participated" (Franklin, 1994, p. 10). But in the late 1980s and into the 1990s, NOMAS committed itself to antiracism work within its organization and to connecting with men of color outside of the organization. As a result, by the mid-1990s, the struggle against racial oppression had become an important part of the political discourse of NOMAS, along with the struggle against sexism and heterosexism. In addition, more men of color were participating as active members and leaders in NOMAS. A disproportionate number of these men of color appear to identify as gay or bisexual, which suggests that the gender and sexual politics of such an organization might not be attractive to most men of color unless they have first faced sexual oppression within their own families or racial and ethnic communities.

Is NOMAS the model for a progressive men's movement? There appear to be two positions on this question among profeminist men. The first position is expressed by R. W. Connell (1995) in the quote that introduces this chapter. Connell argues that the very idea of a "men's movement" is shot through with danger, contradiction, and paradox. White-identified people who want to oppose racism do not form a "white peoples' movement." Heterosexually identified people who want to oppose heterosexism and homophobia do not form a "straight peoples' movement." However, to end racism and heterosexism, white people and heterosexuals *will* have to stand up, speak out, and act within their own families, political groups, workplaces, and communities to oppose oppression and to support progressive change. Similarly, Connell asserts, profeminist men *do* need to educate, counsel, and work with other men to bring about an end to institutionalized sexism. This means that profeminist activism by men will inevitably pit profeminist men against the entrenched interests of other men.

Another view, articulated by longtime NOMAS activist Michael Kimmel (personal communication, April 1996), argues passionately for the need for an organized, profeminist men's movement:

> I agree with Connell that a profeminist men's movement is shot through with contradictions. But so what? What isn't? . . . Politics is invariably messy and contradictory. The idea that there are men who do support feminism and create an organization to spread that word is more than just contradictory. It does something else. It creates a visible organizational pole, a blip on the political screen, to which other people can respond. . . . [It] suggests that there can possibly be some men who do support feminism as men, who support gays and lesbians as straight people, who support people of color as white people. . . . NOMAS has become the pole that attracts the heat. . . . I decided a long time ago that I would rather get messy with the contradictions than remain aloof from real political life. . . . Even men are part of the rainbow, no?

I think NOMAS is an important organization—in fact, I have been a member almost since its inception and have worked as a contributing editor for the NOMAS-sponsored magazine *Changing Men* since the early 1980s. However, I have always seen NOMAS not so much as a "movement" but as a political and educational network. I admire the work that NOMAS men do in their communities to stop violence, to educate about and agitate for equality and justice. But my sense, following Connell (1995), is that profeminist activism among men is best accomplished not through a "men's movement" but in schools, in political parties, in labor unions and professional organizations, in workplaces, in families, and through supportive alliances with feminist and other progressive organizations that are working for social justice. One example of this kind of profeminist activism by men can be seen in the area of sport, in which some men, many of them heterosexuals, are actively teaching about and organizing to confront and change the heterosexism and misogyny within male athletic groups that lead to disproportionately high levels of violence against women by male athletes (e.g., Crosset, Benedict, & McDonald, 1995; Curry, 1991; J. Katz, 1995; McKay, 1991; Sabo, 1994a).

So if men's movement organizations are of limited utility, is there no group or political tendency today that might serve as a nexus for political coalition building? I would argue that today, it is predominantly the discourse of feminist women of color that seems to provide both the critical analysis of "intersecting systems of domination and oppression" as well as to point to the potential for bridge building between and among separate groups. I will conclude with some thoughts on how a profeminist politics among men might find this progressive nexus in what Baca Zinn and Dill (1996) call "multiracial feminism."

Placing Multiracial Feminism
at the Center of Political Discourse

About 3 years ago, I received a call from a representative of the National Organization for Women (NOW) Legal Defense and Education Fund, who was searching for a male academic who would publicly take a stand against the controversial movement in Detroit to establish all-male public schools in predominantly African American districts. "Well," I waffled, "I'm not *for* it, but I do understand how the deteriorating conditions in urban communities and schools and the especially devastating impact on young African American males have led many African Americans to desperately search for solutions." "Yes," the NOW representative replied, "We know that too, but *our* position is that there is no evidence that separating boys from girls is going to solve those problems. In fact, we are worried that this approach ignores the problems faced by African American girls and will justify tipping more educational resources away from them. Would you be willing to testify on behalf of our position?" "Well," I sidestepped and backpedaled, "I really think it's more appropriate that you find African American scholars to talk about this."

In the end, I passed on the opportunity to take a public stand on this issue. My gut-level reason was that I felt it inappropriate for me, a white male academic, to take a public stand against a grassroots initiative in an African American community. But I also felt that in taking no public stand on this issue, I had failed in my commitment to support women's quest for equality. After having spent much of my time in the past few years researching, writing, and teaching about the ways that race, class, gender, and sexual systems of oppression often "intersect," this issue crystallized for me the fact that conceptualizing and theorizing are clearly not enough. Like many people, I have acknowledged that it is necessary to move beyond Marxist class reductionist or radical feminist gender reductionist theories that tend to oversimplify the world by falsely collapsing all forms of oppression into one supposedly "primary" cause. Instead, the current movement in progressive sociology is toward theories that conceptualize multiple, semiautonomous, cross-cutting systems of inequality (Baca Zinn et al., 1986; Collins, 1990; Baca Zinn & Dill, 1996). Thus far, though, most attempts at grand theories of these interrelated systems of power, or even more modest conceptual efforts (e.g., Messner & Sabo, 1990), tend to fall short of the task. One reason is that these models tend to assume—altogether too optimistically—that different forms of oppression are part of the same social or cultural dynamic. As a result of this oversimplification, they also tend to assume an underlying congruence of interests, goals, and strategies among the various movements that struggle against these forms of oppression. But when progressive movements perceive their interests as conflicting—as happened in the Detroit case, in which an African American community attempting to take control of its schools came into conflict with feminists—our theories are revealed to be inadequate.

When facing these same complex realities, some postmodernists have argued that modernity has collapsed and with it has evaporated the hope for a transcendent "historical subject" (be it the working class, women, colonized people, etc.) that can attain a conscious grasp of the totality of social life, organize, and act to change it. Within the postmodern view (e.g., Lemert, 1994), a sociologist who asserts that her or his work is operating from the standpoint of a commitment to social justice is scoffed at as hopelessly mired in passé, modernist thought. Instead, postmodernists argue, we face an increasingly unstable and fragmented world in which knowledge can be, at best, only partial and groups can coalesce only temporarily around limited and short-term goals.

I agree that the world is complex. In fact, the idea of a single, transcendent revolutionary historical subject (such as the working class or women) that can understand and change the totality of social life was probably always an incorrect and naive assumption made by revolutionary intellectuals. "The working class" and "women" have always been internally differentiated and fragmented groups that, respectively, Marxists and some feminists have falsely universalized. However, I would argue that to abandon the project of human liberation now is to engage in an act of historical capitulation to the forces of greed, violence, and oppression, right at a time in history when new social movements have achieved partial (sometimes even dramatic) successes in decolonization, women's rights, gay and lesbian liberation, and antiracism. But as Todd Gitlin (1995) has recently pointed out, any movement for progressive institutional change will have to transcend the destructive tendency of these new social movements to engage in narrow, single-issue identity politics that set them against each other. For this to happen, various groups must coalesce around a "common dream" of equality and social justice.

At this historical moment in the United States, I believe that the greatest potential force for serving as a nexus through which progressive discourses and practices can link up to broaden the push for such a "common dream" of social justice is what Baca Zinn and Dill (1996) have called "multiracial feminism." This approach attempts to take into account, simultaneously, a structural analysis of power and inequality with an appreciation of and respect for difference. Take, for example, some of the key issues that I discussed in Chapter 5 that are being raised today about black masculinity within racial discourses in politics and popular culture. The current Afrocentric movement is surely not in the tradition of Martin Luther King's calls for racial integration. Instead, it echoes Malcolm X's calls for community autonomy. And just as was true of the Muslim and Black Power movements of the 1960s, central to Afrocentrism today is a militant assertion of "black manhood." This concern was depicted in the popular film *Boyz 'n the Hood*. The film suggests that the young males in the 'hood are faced with two major options. The first one is to follow the lead of the young hoodlum "new heads" and likely end up cycling in and out of prison and eventually getting killed at a young age. A second possibility is suggested in the case of the talented young football player who is being recruited by the University of Southern California. This option, too, is revealed as a dead end, as the youth's talents and dreams cannot safeguard him from the violence in his community. But *Boyz 'n the Hood* offers a ray of hope. Here, for one of the very few times in American cinema, a positive image of an African American father was presented. The son of this father, we see, eventually makes the right choices that allow him to escape the violent 'hood and attend college. This was undoubtedly a positive message in some ways, but in other ways this film raised the same troubling question that the Detroit all-male schools issue raised: What about the women? To make its point that a strong father is the answer to the problem of black male youth, the film went about depicting mothers as either irresponsible crack addicts, unfair bitches, or upwardly mobile professionals who neglect their children for their careers.

Twenty years ago, the masculinist gender politics of antiracism organizations were rarely questioned. The few black feminists such as Michelle Wallace (1978), who challenged assumptions of male superiority by leaders such as Eldridge Cleaver or Stokely Carmichael, were accused of undermining the cause of black liberation by dividing women from men. Today, with assertions of black manhood again taking center stage in Afrocentric discourse and political practice, there is a broader, more assertive and sophisticated response from black women. For example, a few years ago I attended a session on black males at the American Sociological Association meetings, where Elijah Anderson (1990) presented some of the findings of his ethnographic research that later became *Streetwise*. Anderson told the following story, based on the narrative of a black man, of a late-night street interaction between three black males and a white woman:

> A white lady walkin' down the street with a pocketbook. She start walkin' fast. She get so paranoid she break into a little stride. Me and my friends comin' from a party about 12:00. She stops and goes up on the porch of a house, but you could tell she didn't live there. I stop and say, "Miss, you didn't have to do that. I thought you might think we're some wolf pack. I'm twenty-eight, he's twenty-six, he's twenty-nine. You ain't gotta run from us." She said, "Well, I'm sorry." I said, "You can come down. I know you don't live there. We just comin' from a party." We just walked down the street and she came back down, walked across the street where she really wanted to go. So she tried to act as though she lived there. And she didn't. After we said, "You ain't gotta run from us," she said, "No, I was really in a hurry." My boy said, "No you wasn't. You thought we was gon' snatch yo' pocketbook." We pulled money out. "See this, we work." I said, "We grown men, now. You gotta worry about them fifteen-, sixteen-, seventeen-year-old boys. That's what you worry about. But we're grown men." I told her all this. "They the ones ain't got no jobs; they're too young to really work. They're the ones you worry about, not us." She understood that. You could tell she was relieved and she gave a sigh. She came back down the steps, even went across the street. (pp. 167-168)

The point of Anderson's story—that in public places, black males are commonly unfairly suspected of being violent rapists—was well taken. But the woman in the story was a somewhat humorous prop for making this point about the indignities that black males face. Anderson did not appear to have much empathy for her. As he finished telling the story, a white woman sitting in front of me whispered to the white woman next to her, "He acts like she had no reason to be frightened of a pack of men. Of *course* she was scared! Women are attacked and raped every day!" It seemed clear to me that this woman identified and empathized with the white woman in the story but gave no indication that she understood Anderson's point about the impact of this omnipresent suspicion on the vast majority of black males who do not rape. After the talk, during the discussion session, an African American woman stood up and bridged this chasm by eloquently empathizing with the legitimate fears of the woman *and* with the cumulative public humiliation of the black males in the story. The woman *and* the men in this story, she asserted, were differentially victimized in public space. The solution lies in their learning to empathize with each other and then building from that common empathy a movement that fights against the oppressive system that dehumanizes them both.

This scene, it seemed to me, demonstrated both the limits of masculinist Afrocentrism and of white feminism and the role that multiracial feminism can play in creating new standpoints that bridge these two movements. As Patricia Hill Collins (1990) has so eloquently put it, black women are often "outsiders within"—as women, they are outsiders within the male dominated Afrocentric movement; as blacks, they are outsiders within white-dominated feminism. Their social positions "on the margins," to use bell hooks's (1984) terminology, give black women (and by implication, other women of color) unique standpoints through which the complex mechanisms and interweavings of power and oppression can be more clearly deconstructed and, possibly, resisted. From a multiracial feminist standpoint, African American males' unique experiences of oppression are acknowledged and struggled against. But multiracial feminists do not accept the analysis presented by some men of color (e.g., Peña, 1991; Staples, 1995b) that interprets public displays of misogyny, rape, and other forms of violence against women by men of color primarily as distorted or displaced responses to racism and to class constraints. Instead, gender must be viewed *not* as a "superstructural" manifestation of class and/or racial politics but as a semi-autonomous system of power relations between women and men (Baca Zinn et al., 1986; Collins, 1990).

In an essay on black masculinity, bell hooks (1992) charges that what she calls "conservative Afrocentric males" often draw on "phallocentric masculinity" as a resource to fight racial oppression. She observes that public figures such as Eddie Murphy and Spike Lee tend to exploit the commodification of phallocentric black masculinity. But, hooks argues, there exist also what she calls "progressive Afrocentric males," including many gay black men, who are, in her words, "not sitting around worried about castration and emasculation" (p. 102); instead they are exploring more egalitarian relationships with women and with other men.

Bridges to the Terrain of Progressive Coalition Building

Some men and women are clearly already working within the terrain of progressive coalition building. In Figure 6.1, I separate that terrain from the other three areas with a dotted line, rather than a solid line, to emphasize the permeable nature of the boundaries I have described. In fact, there are several groups of men and women who are currently constructing discourses and practices that might "bridge" otherwise more narrowly defined groups into the terrain of multiracial feminism and progressive coalition building. Clearly, we can expect very few men to move from the terrain of antifeminist backlash to multiracial feminism. On the other hand, the fact that some men are struggling to understand and overcome the "costs" of masculinity creates a potential opening for the development of a more fundamental critical analysis of hegemonic masculinity—including an understanding of how the costs of masculinity are linked to men's institutional power. The men who are most likely to serve as a bridge from the terrain of antifeminist backlash to the terrain of progressive coalition building are the fragments of the mythopoetic men's movement who are currently engaged in dialogues with profeminist men.

Radical profeminist men who are working within the terrain of antipatriarchal politics are often engaged in extremely important work. Their powerfully charged call for men to renounce masculinity clearly resonates with some men. And some of their educational and political actions to stop male violence support women who are working to make the world a safer place for women. The fact that they might convince even a few men to stop being violent against women is an invaluable contribution in and of itself. On the other hand, for reasons that I discussed in Chapter 4, radical feminist men are more likely to engage in a more insular and limited antipatriarchal politics than they are to engage in bridge building with other groups who do not necessarily share their analysis and assumptions about the centrality of male sexuality in the oppression of women and of other men.

By comparison, there is far greater potential for movement from the terrain of racial and sexual identity politics into the terrain of progressive coalition building. For instance, some African American men who have worked within a socialist framework, such as Manning Marable (1994) and Cornel West (1993), appear to be formulating a feminist-informed critique of hegemonic masculinity within their race and class political program. Similarly, profeminist gay men continue to provide bridges between feminist women, gay liberation, and profeminist men's organizations. And especially, gay men of color (e.g., Almaguer, 1991; Cochran & Mays, 1995; Leong, 1996; Mercer & Julien, 1988) are in the forefront of attempts to integrate a critical understanding of the interrelationships between race, class, gender, and sexual systems of oppression. I would speculate that this is because gay men of color are also likely to experience themselves as "outsiders within" in multiple ways. In their own racial and ethnic communities, they may be shunned (or worse) due to ingrained homophobia; within gay communities, they may be marginalized (or worse) because of racism. As a result of this multiple marginality, gay men of color hold the potential to bridge gay and lesbian liberation, antiracism movements, and feminist organizations into powerful coalitions (Takagi, 1996).

I believe that it would be most fruitful for those who are engaged in progressive politics—both academics and movement activists—to listen to the public conversations taking place today between gay men of color, progressive men of color, and feminist women of color. An example of this conversation can be found in bell hooks's dialogue with Cornel West (hooks & West, 1991). Theory construction is under way in these conversations. One promise that these conversations hold is that even those of us who are not central players (and here I am thinking particularly but not exclusively of people such as myself who identify as "white," as "heterosexual," as "middle-class," and as "men") can listen in and learn to ask new, critical questions. Decentered theoretically, we can begin to turn commonly asked questions back on themselves: not, Why do black men so often misbehave? rather, Why are we so *obsessed* with this question and what, in fact, about the everyday misbehaviors of *white* men and *middle- and upper-class* men? The invisible presence in Elijah Anderson's street scene, discussed earlier, are the powerful upper-class white men, who, through their control of institutions, have removed jobs from the inner cities, cut aid to schools, and allowed police protection for citizens to deteriorate. Simultaneously, some police engaged in racist terror tactics and refused to take the measures that might make public life safe for women, thus imposing a *de facto* curfew on them. But privileged males are invisible in this story because the race, class, and gendered power of these males are attached to their positions in institutions, not to their personal behaviors in the street. In fact, their everyday actions in political, corporate, or educational institutions are commonly defined as "normal" male behavior.

The task of a sociology of masculinities, it seems to me, is to raise critical questions about the "normal" operation of hegemonic masculinity in such a way that these actions are redefined as "misbehaviors." I am convinced that today the conversations taking place within multiracial feminism offer us the best (though not a perfect, complete, or total) theoretical framework through which we might better begin to understand and confront the crucial issues of our day. Multiracial feminism invites us to shift our attention away from simplistic bickering between oppressed groups and, instead, to focus our energies on developing a critical understanding of the complex relations of power that structure our social realities. It is really beyond belief to imagine that a group made up primarily or exclusively of white, class-privileged, and heterosexual men could or would ever develop such a radically progressive standpoint. In fact, I would argue that NOMAS, a group made up primarily of men, has been moving in these sorts of progressive directions in recent years precisely because its members have been listening to—and attempting to develop a practice in relation to—multiracial feminism. This organization starts with the assumption that men—even men from the most privileged class, racial, and sexual groups—can participate and contribute to movements for social justice. To make such a contribution will mean that men will have to work against our own narrowly defined economic and political interests. But men also have a stake in the movement for social justice. In rejecting hegemonic masculinity and its rewards, we also may become more fully human. For I am convinced that the humanization of men is intricately intertwined with the empowerment of women.

Adam, B. D. (1977). A social history of gay politics. In M. P. Levine (Ed.), *Gay men: The sociology of male homosexuality* (pp. 285-300). New York: Harper & Row.

Adam, B. D. (1995). *The rise of a gay and lesbian movement.* New York: Twayne.

Adams, M. (1985). Child of the glacier. In F. Baumli (Ed.), *Men freeing men: Exploding the myth of the traditional male* (pp. 5-18). Jersey City, NJ: New Atlantis.

Allen, M. (1995). We've come a long way too, baby. And we've still got a ways to go. So give us a break! In M. S. Kimmel (Ed.), *The politics of manhood: Profeminist men respond to the mythopoetic men's movement (and the mythopoetic leaders answer)* (pp. 308-312). Philadelphia: Temple University Press.

Allen, R. (1995). Racism, sexism and a million men. *The Black Scholar, 25,* 24-26.

Almaguer, T. (1991). Chicano men: A cartography of homosexual identity and behavior. *Differences: A Journal of Feminist Cultural Studies, 3,* 75-100.

Altman, D. (1982). *The homosexualization of America.* Boston: Beacon.

Andersen, D. (1977). Warren the success object. In J. Snodgrass (Ed.), *For men against sexism* (pp. 146-149). Albion, CA: Times Change Press.

Anderson, E. (1990). *Streetwise: Race, class, and change in an urban community.* Chicago: University of Chicago Press.

Arendell, T. (1992). After divorce: Investigations into father absence. *Gender & Society, 6,* 562-586.

Arendell, T. (1995). *Fathers and divorce.* Thousand Oaks, CA: Sage.

Baca Zinn, M. (1982). Chicano men and masculinity. *Journal of Ethnic Studies, 10,* 29-44.

Baca Zinn, M., Cannon, L. W., Higgenbotham, E., & Dill, B. T. (1986). The costs of exclusionary practices in women's studies. *Signs: Journal of Women in Culture and Society, 11,* 290-303.

111

Baca Zinn, M., & Dill, B. T. (1996). Theorizing difference from multiracial feminism. *Feminist Studies 22*, 321-331.

Balswick, J., & Peek, C. (1971). The inexpressive male: A tragedy of American society. *The Family Coordinator, 20*, 363-368.

Baumli, F. (Ed.). (1985). *Men freeing men: Exploding the myth of the traditional male.* Jersey City, NJ: New Atlantis.

Beal, B., & Gray, J. (1995, March). *Bill McCartney and the Promise Keepers: Exploring the connections among sport, Christianity, and masculinity.* Paper presented at the annual meeting of the American Alliance for Health, Physical Education, Recreation and Dance, Portland, OR.

Bertoia, C. E., & Drakich, J. (1995). The fathers' rights movement: Contradictions in rhetoric and practice. In W. Marsiglio (Ed.), *Fatherhood: Contemporary theory, research, and social policy* (pp. 230-254). Thousand Oaks, CA: Sage.

Blauner, B. (1996). Review of *Masculinities*, by R. W. Connell. *Contemporary Sociology, 25*, 166-168.

Bliss, S. (1995). Mythopoetic men's movements. In M. S. Kimmel (Ed.), *The politics of manhood: Profeminist men respond to the mythopoetic men's movement (and the mythopoetic leaders answer)* (pp. 292-308). Philadelphia: Temple University Press.

Blum, L. (1991). *Between feminism and labor: The significance of the comparable worth movement.* Berkeley: University of California Press.

Bly, R. (1990). *Iron John: A book about men.* Reading, MA: Addison-Wesley.

Bly, R. (1995). Thoughts on reading this book. In M. S. Kimmel (Ed.), *The politics of manhood: Profeminist men respond to the mythopoetic men's movement (and the mythopoetic leaders answer)* (pp. 271-274). Philadelphia: Temple University Press.

Bowser, B. P. (1994). Black men and AIDS: Prevention and black sexuality. In R. G. Majors & J. U. Gordon (Eds.), *The American black male* (pp. 115-126). Chicago: Nelson-Hall.

Boyd, H. (1995). The march. *The Black Scholar, 25*, 12-16.

Brannon, R. (1976). The male sex role: Our culture's blueprint of manhood, and what it's done for us lately. In D. S. David & R. Brannon (Eds.), *The forty-nine percent majority: The male sex role* (pp. 1-45). Reading, MA: Addison-Wesley.

Brannon, R. (1981-1982, Winter). Are the "Free Men" a faction of our movement? *M: Gentle Men for Gender Justice, 7.*

Brod, H. (1983-1984). Work clothes and leisure suits: The class basis and bias of the men's movement. *M: Gentle Men for Gender Justice, 11*, 10-12, 38-40.

Brod, H. (1984). Eros thanatized: Pornography and male sexuality. *Humanities in Society, 7*, 47-63.

Brod, H. (Ed.). (1987). *The making of masculinities: The new men's studies.* Boston: Allen & Unwin.

Canada, G. (1995). *Fist stick knife gun: A personal history of violence in America.* Boston: Beacon.

Carrier, J. (1992). Miguel: Sexual life history of a gay Mexican American. In G. Herdt (Ed.), *Gay culture in America: Essays from the field* (pp. 202-224). Boston: Beacon.

Carrigan, T., Connell, B., & Lee, J. (1987). Toward a new sociology of masculinity. In H. Brod (Ed.), *The making of masculinities: The new men's studies* (pp. 63-100). Boston: Allen & Unwin.

Clark, C. (1990). Pornography without power? In M. S. Kimmel (Ed.), *Men confront pornography* (pp. 281-284). New York: Crown.

Clarke, S. A. (1991). Fear of a black planet. *Socialist Review, 21,* 37-59.

Clatterbaugh, K. (1990). *Contemporary perspectives on masculinity: Men, women, and politics in modern society.* Boulder, CO: Westview.

Clawson, M. A. (1989). *Constructing brotherhood: Class, gender, and fraternalism.* Princeton, NJ: Princeton University Press.

Cleaver, E. (1965). *Soul on ice.* New York: McGraw-Hill.

Coakley, J. (1993). *The Promise Keepers national men's conference: The cutting edge?* Unpublished manuscript, University of Colorado at Colorado Springs.

Cochran, S. D., & Mays, V. M. (1995). Sociocultural facets of the black gay male experience. In M. S. Kimmel & M. A. Messner (Eds.), *Men's lives* (3rd ed., pp. 432-439). Boston: Allyn & Bacon.

Cole, E. L. (1982). *Maximized manhood: A guide to family survival.* Springdale, PA: Whitaker House.

Collins, P. H. (1990). *Black feminist thought: Knowledge, consciousness, and the politics of empowerment.* Boston: Unwin Hyman.

Collinson, D. L. (1988). "Engineering humor": Masculinity, joking, and conflict in shop-floor relations. *Organization Studies, 9,* 181-199.

Coltrane, S. (1989). Household labor and the routine production of gender. *Social Problems, 36,* 473-490.

Coltrane, S. (1995). The future of fatherhood: Social, demographic, and economic influences on men's family involvements. In W. Marsiglio (Ed.), *Fatherhood: Contemporary theory, research, and social policy* (pp. 255-274). Thousand Oaks, CA: Sage.

Coltrane, S. (1996). *Family man: Fatherhood, housework and gender equity.* Oxford, UK: Oxford University Press.

Coltrane, S., & Hickman, N. (1992). The rhetoric of rights and needs: Moral discourse in the reform of child custody and child support laws. *Social Problems, 39,* 400-420.

Connell, R. W. (1987). *Gender and power.* Stanford, CA: Stanford University Press.

Connell, R. W. (1991). *Men of reason: Themes of rationality and change in the lives of men in the new professions.* Unpublished manuscript.

Connell, R. W. (1992). Drumming up the wrong tree. *Tikkun, 7,* 517-530.

Connell, R. W. (1993). The big picture: Masculinities in recent world history. *Theory and Society, 22,* 597-624.

Connell, R. W. (1995). *Masculinities.* Berkeley: University of California Press.

Crosset, T., Benedict, J. R., & McDonald, M. A. (1995). Male student-athletes reported for sexual assault: A survey of campus police departments and judicial affairs offices. *Journal of Sport and Social Issues, 19,* 126-140.

Curry, T. J. (1991). Fraternal bonding in the locker room: A profeminist analysis of talk about competition and women. *Sociology of Sport Journal, 8,* 119-135.

Daniels, R. (1996, January). The promise of the Million Man March. *Z Magazine,* pp. 21-23.

Dansky, S., Knoebel, J., & Pitchford, K. (1977). The effeminist manifesto. In J. Snodgrass (Ed.), *For men against sexism* (pp. 116-120). Albion, CA: Times Change Press.

Dash, M. (1995). Betwixt and between in the men's movement. In M. S. Kimmel (Ed.), *The politics of manhood: Profeminist men respond to the mythopoetic men's movement (and the mythopoetic leaders answer)* (pp. 355-361). Philadelphia: Temple University Press.

Davis, A. (1981). *Woman, race and class.* New York: Vintage Books.

D'Emilio, J. (1992). Women against pornography: Feminist frontier or social purity crusade? In J. D'Emilio (Ed.), *Making trouble: Essays on gay history, politics and the university* (pp. 202-215). New York: Routledge.

Dowsett, D. W. (1993). I'll show you mine, if you show me yours: Gay men, masculinity research, men's studies and sex. *Theory and Society, 22,* 697-710.

Doyle, R. (1985). Divorce. In F. Baumli (Ed.), *Men freeing men: Exploding the myth of the traditional male* (p. 166). Jersey City, NJ: New Atlantis.

Echols, A. (1989). *Daring to be bad: Radical feminism in America, 1967-1975.* Minneapolis: University of Minnesota Press.

Edwards, T. (1990). Beyond sex and gender: Masculinity, homosexuality and social theory. In J. Hearn & D. Morgan (Eds.), *Masculinities and social theory* (pp. 110-123). Boston: Unwin Hyman.

Ehrenreich, B. (1983). *The hearts of men: American dreams and the flight from commitment.* New York: Anchor/Doubleday.

Eisenstein, Z. R. (Ed.). (1979). *Capitalist patriarchy and the case for socialist feminism.* New York: Monthly Review Press.

Esterberg, K. G. (1994). From accommodation to liberation: A social movement analysis of lesbians in the homophile movement. *Gender & Society, 8,* 424-443.

Evans, T. (1994). Spiritual purity. In *Seven promises of a promise keeper* (pp. 73-81). Colorado Springs, CO: Focus on the Family.

Faludi, S. (1991). *Backlash: The undeclared war against American women.* New York: Crown.

Falwell, J. (Ed.). (1981). *How you can help clean up America.* Washington, DC: Moral Majority.

Fanon, F. (1970). *Black skin, white masks.* London: Paladin.

Farrell, W. (1974). *The liberated man.* New York: Random House.

Farrell, W. (1993). *The myth of male power: Why men are the disposable sex.* New York: Simon & Schuster.

Fasteau, M. F. (1974). *The male machine.* New York: McGraw-Hill.

Fausto-Sterling, A. (1985). *Myths of gender: Biological theories about men and women.* New York: Basic Books.

Filene, P. (1975). *Him/her/self: Sex roles in modern America.* New York: Harcourt Brace Jovanovich.

Fong-Torres, B. (1995). Why are there no male Asian anchor men on TV? In M. S. Kimmel & M. A. Messner (Eds.), *Men's lives* (3rd ed., pp. 208-211). Boston: Allyn & Bacon.

Frankenberg, R. (1993). *White women, race matters: The social construction of whiteness.* Minneapolis: University of Minnesota Press.

Franklin, C. W., II. (1987). Surviving the institutional decimation of black males: Causes, consequences, and intervention. In H. Brod (Ed.), *The making of masculinities* (pp. 155-169). Boston: Allyn & Unwin.

Franklin, C. W., II. (1994). Men's studies, the men's movement, and the study of black masculinities: Further demystification of masculinities in America. In R. G. Majors & J. U. Gordon (Eds.), *The American black male* (pp. 3-20). Chicago: Nelson-Hall.

Franzway, S., Court, D., & Connell, R. W. (1989). *Staking a claim: Feminism, bureaucracy and the state.* Sydney, Australia: Allyn & Unwin.

Freire, P. (1970). *Pedagogy of the oppressed.* New York: Herden & Herden.

Fung, R. (1996). Looking for my penis: The eroticized Asian in gay video porn. In R. Leong (Ed.), *Asian American sexualities: Dimensions of the gay and lesbian experience* (pp. 181-198). New York: Routledge.

Gerschick, T. J., & Miller, A. S. (1995). Coming to terms: Masculinity and physical disability. In M. S. Kimmel & M. A. Messner (Eds.), *Men's lives* (3rd ed., pp. 262-276). Boston: Allyn & Bacon.

Gerzon, M. (1982). *A choice of heroes: The changing faces of America's manhood.* Boston: Houghton Mifflin.

Gibbs, J. T. (Ed.). (1988). *Young, black, and male in America: An endangered species.* Dover, MA: Auburn House.

Gibbs, J. T. (1994). Anger in young black males: Victims or victimizers? In R. G. Majors & J. U. Gordon (Eds.), *The American black male* (pp. 127-144). Chicago: Nelson-Hall.

Gilder, G. (1973). *Sexual suicide.* New York: Bantam.

Gilder, G. (1981). *Wealth and poverty.* New York: Basic Books.

Gilkas, C. T. (1985). Together in harness: Women's traditions in the sanctified church. *Signs, 10,* 669-678.

Gitlin, T. (1995). *The twilight of common dreams: Why America is wracked by culture wars.* New York: Metropolitan Books.

Goldberg, H. (1976). *The hazards of being male: Surviving the myth of masculine privilege.* New York: Signet.

Goldberg, H. (1979). *The new male: From macho to sensitive but still all male.* New York: Signet.

Goldberg, S. (1974). *The inevitability of patriarchy.* New York: William Morrow.

Gordon, L. R. (1995). Race and racism in the last quarter of '95: The OJ and post-OJ trial & the Million Man March. *The Black Scholar, 25,* 37-58.

Gray, S. (1987). Sharing the shop floor. In M. Kaufman (Ed.), *Beyond patriarchy: Essays by men on pleasure, power, and change* (pp. 216-234). Toronto: Oxford University Press.

Haddad, R. (1985). Concepts and overview of the men's liberation movement. In F. Baumli (Ed.), *Men freeing men: Exploding the myth of the traditional male* (pp. 281-288). Jersey City, NJ: New Atlantis.

Hagan, K. L. (Ed.). (1992). *Women respond to the men's movement.* New York: Pandora/Harper Collins.

Hanisch, C. (1975). Men's liberation. In Redstockings (Ed.), *Feminist revolution* (pp. 72-76). New York: Random House.

Hansen, K. V. (1986). Women's unions and the search for a political identity. *Socialist Review, 86,* 67-95.

Hansen, K. V., & Philipson, I. J., (Eds.). (1990). *Women, class, and the feminist imagination: A socialist-feminist reader.* Philadelphia: Temple University Press.

Hantover, J. P. (1978). The Boy Scouts and the validation of masculinity. *Journal of Social Issues, 34*(1), 184-195.

Hare, N. (1971). Will the real black man please stand up? *The Black Scholar, 2,* 32-35.

Hare, N., & Hare, J. (1984). *The endangered black family: Coping with the unisexualization and coming extinction of the black race.* San Francisco: Black Think Tank.

Harrison, J., Chin, J., & Ficarratto, T. (1995). Warning: Masculinity may be dangerous to your health. In M. S. Kimmel & M. A. Messner (Eds.), *Men's lives* (3rd ed., pp. 237-249). Boston: Allyn & Bacon.

Hartley, R. E. (1959). Sex role pressures in the socialization of the male child. *Psychological Reports, 5,* 457-468.

Hartmann, H. (1976). Capitalism, patriarchy, and job segregation by sex. *Signs: Journal of Women in Culture and Society, 1,* 137-169.

Hartmann, H. (1981). The unhappy marriage of Marxism and feminism. In L. Sargent (Ed.), *Women and revolution* (pp. 1-41). Boston: South End.

Henley, N. (1970). Male chauvinism: Attitudes and practices. *Newsletter of the New University Conference,* p. 1.

Herek, G. M. (1991). Psychological heterosexism and anti-gay violence: The social psychology of bigotry and bashing. In G. M. Herek & K. Berrill (Eds.), *Hate crimes* (pp. 149-169). Newbury Park, CA: Sage.

Hertz, R. (1986). *More equal than others: Women and men in dual career marriages.* Berkeley: University of California Press.

Hess, B. B., & Ferree, M. M. (Eds.). (1988). *Analyzing gender.* Newbury Park, CA: Sage.

Hoch, P. (1979). *White hero, black beast: Racism, sexism and the mask of masculinity.* London: Pluto.

Hochschild, A. (1989). *The second shift: Working parents and the revolution at home.* New York: Viking.

Hondagneu-Sotelo, P. (1992). Overcoming patriarchal constraints: The reconstruction of gender relations among Mexican immigrant women and men. *Gender & Society, 6,* 393-415.

Hondagneu-Sotelo, P., & Messner, M. A. (1994). Gender displays and men's power: The "new man" and the Mexican immigrant man. In H. Brod & M. Kaufman (Eds.), *Theorizing masculinities* (pp. 200-218). Thousand Oaks, CA: Sage.

hooks, b. (1984). *Feminist theory: From margin to center.* Boston: South End.

hooks, b. (1992). Reconstructing black masculinity. In b. hooks, *Black looks: Race and representation* (pp. 87-114). Boston: South End.

hooks, b., & West, C. (1991). *Breaking bread: Insurgent black intellectual life.* Boston: South End.

Jones, B. E., & Christmas, V. P. (1994). African-American males and homelessness. In R. G. Majors & J. U. Gordon (Eds.), *The American black male* (pp. 105-114). Chicago: Nelson-Hall.

Kandiyoti, D. (1988). Bargaining with patriarchy. *Gender & Society, 2,* 274-290.

Kann, M. E. (1986). The costs of being on top. *Journal of the National Association for Women Deans, Administrators, & Counselors, 49,* 29-37.

Karenga, M. (1995). The Million Man March/Day of Absence mission statement. *The Black Scholar, 25,* 2-11.

Katz, J. (1995). Reconstructing masculinity in the locker room: The mentors in violence prevention project. *Harvard Educational Review, 65,* 163-174.

Katz, J. N. (1995). *The invention of heterosexuality.* New York: Dutton.

Kaufman, D. (1987). Coming home to Jewish orthodoxy: Reactionary or radical women? *Tikkun, 2,* 60-63.

Kaufman, M. (1993). *Cracking the armour: Power, pain and the lives of men.* New York : Viking.

Keen, S. (1991). *Fire in the belly: On being a man.* New York: Bantam.

Kemper, T. D. (1990). *Social structure and testosterone: Explorations of the socio-bio-social chain.* New Brunswick, NJ: Rutgers University Press.

Kimmel, M. S. (Ed.). (1987a). *Changing men: New directions in research on men and masculinity.* Newbury Park, CA: Sage.

Kimmel, M. S. (1987b). Men's responses to feminism at the turn of the century. *Gender & Society, 1*(3), 261-283.

Kimmel, M. S. (1990). "Insult" or "injury": Sex, pornography, and sexism. In M. S. Kimmel (Ed.), *Men confront pornography* (pp. 305-319). New York: Crown.

Kimmel, M. S. (1992). Reading men: Men, masculinity, and publishing. *Contemporary Sociology, 21,* 162-171.

Kimmel, M. S. (1995a). Afterword. In M. S. Kimmel (Ed.), *The politics of manhood: Profeminist men respond to the mythopoetic men's movement (and the mythopoetic leaders answer)* (pp. 362-374). Philadelphia: Temple University Press.

Kimmel, M. S. (Ed.). (1995b). *The politics of manhood: Profeminist men respond to the mythopoetic men's movement (and the mythopoetic leaders answer).* Philadelphia: Temple University Press.

Kimmel, M. S. (1996). *Manhood in America: A cultural history.* New York: Free Press.

Kimmel, M. S., & Kaufman, M. (1994). Weekend warriors: The new men's movement. In H. Brod & M. Kaufman (Eds.), *Theorizing masculinities* (pp. 259-288). Thousand Oaks, CA: Sage.

Kimmel, M. S., & Messner, M. A. (Eds.). (1989). *Men's lives.* New York: Macmillan.

Kimmel, M. S., & Messner, M. A. (Eds.). (1995). *Men's lives* (3rd ed.). Boston: Allyn & Bacon.

Kimmel, M. S., & Mosmiller, T. E. (1992). *Against the tide: Pro-feminist men in the United States, a documentary history.* Boston: Beacon.

Kipnis, A. (1995). The profeminist men's movement. In M. S. Kimmel (Ed.), *The politics of manhood: Profeminist men respond to the mythopoetic men's movement (and the mythopoetic leaders answer)* (pp. 275-286). Philadelphia: Temple University Press.

Kivel, P. (1992). *Men's work: How to stop the violence that tears our lives apart.* Center City, MN: Hazelden.

Klein, A. M. (1993). *Little big men: Bodybuilding subculture and gender construction.* Albany: State University of New York Press.

Komarovsky, M. (1992). The concept of social role revisited. *Gender & Society, 6,* 301-313.

Kopay, D., & Young, P. D. (1977). *The David Kopay story.* New York: Arbor House.

Kunjufu, J. (1985). *Countering the conspiracy to destroy black boys.* Chicago: African American Images.

La Rossa, R. (1988). Fatherhood and social change. *Family Relations, 37,* 451-457.

Lefkowitz-Horowitz, H. (1987). *Campus life: Undergraduate cultures from the end of the eighteenth century to the present.* New York: Knopf.

Leibowitz, E. (1996, May 31-June 6). Million man mea culpa: The Promise Keepers' plan for Christian male redemption. *LA Weekly,* pp. 22-25.

Lemert, C. (1994). Subjectivity's limit: The unsolved riddle of the standpoint. *Sociological Theory, 10,* 63-72.

Leong, R. (1996). Introduction: Home bodies and the body politic. In R. Leong (Ed.), *Asian American sexualities: Dimensions of the gay and lesbian experience* (pp. 1-18). New York: Routledge.

Lewis, C. (1986). *Becoming a father.* Milton Keynes, UK: Open University Press.

Lienesch, M. (1990). Anxious patriarchs: Authority and the meaning of masculinity in Christian conservative thought. *Journal of American Culture, 13,* 47-53.

Litewka, J. (1977). The socialized penis. In J. Snodgrass (Ed.), *For men against sexism* (pp. 16-35). Albion, CA: Times Change Press.

Logan, D. (1985). Men abused by women. In F. Baumli (Ed.), *Men freeing men: Exploding the myth of the traditional male* (p. 213). Jersey City, NJ: New Atlantis.

Maccoby, E. E., & Jacklin, C. N. (1975). *The psychology of sex differences.* Stanford, CA: Stanford University Press.

Machung, A. (1989). Talking career, thinking job: Gender differences in career and family expectations of Berkeley seniors. *Feminist Studies, 15,* 35-58.

Majors, R. G. (1994). Conclusion and recommendations: A reason for hope—An overview of the new black movement in the United States. In R. G. Majors & J. U. Gordon (Eds.), *The American black male* (pp. 299-316). Chicago: Nelson-Hall.

Majors, R. G. (1995). Cool pose: The proud signature of black survival. In M. S. Kimmel & M. A. Messner (Eds.), *Men's lives* (3rd ed., pp. 82-85). Boston: Allyn & Bacon.

Majors, R. G., Tyler, R., Peden, B., & Hall, R. (1994). Cool pose: A symbolic mechanism for masculine role enactment and coping by black males. In R. G. Majors & J. U. Gordon (Eds.), *The American black male* (pp. 245-260). Chicago: Nelson-Hall.

Marable, M. (1994). The black male: Searching beyond stereotypes. In R. G. Majors & J. U. Gordon (Eds.), *The American black male* (pp. 69-77). Chicago: Nelson-Hall.

Mauer, M. (1994). A generation behind bars: Black males and the criminal justice system. In R. G. Majors & J. U. Gordon (Eds.), *The American black male* (pp. 81-94). Chicago: Nelson-Hall.

McCartney, B. (1992). It's time for men to take a stand. In B. McCartney (Ed.), *What makes a man? The 12 promises that will change your life* (pp. 9-14). Colorado Springs, CO: NavPress.

McKay, J. (1991). *No pain, no gain? Sport and Australian culture.* Englewood Cliffs, NJ: Prentice Hall.

Men's Consciousness-Raising Group. (1971). *Unbecoming men.* Albion, CA: Times Change Press.

Mercer, K., & Julien, I. (1988). Race, sexual politics and black masculinity: A dossier. In R. Chapman & J. Rutherford (Eds.), *Male order* (p. 112). London: Lawrence & Wishart.

Messner, M. A. (1990). Men studying masculinity: Some epistemological questions in sport sociology. *Sociology of Sport Journal, 7*(2), 136-153.

Messner, M. A. (1992). *Power at play: Sports and the problem of masculinity.* Boston: Beacon.

Messner, M. A. (1993a). "Changing men" and feminist politics in the United States. *Theory & Society, 22*, 723-738.

Messner, M. A. (1993b). Confronting diversity issues in courses on men and masculinity. *Masculinities, 1*, 13-16.

Messner, M. A. (1994). Gay athletes and the gay games: An interview with Tom Waddell. In M. A. Messner & D. F. Sabo (Eds.), *Sex, violence, and power in sports: Rethinking masculinity* (pp. 113-119). Freedom, CA: Crossing Press.

Messner, M. A., & Sabo, D. F. (1990). Toward a critical feminist reappraisal of sport, men and the gender order. In M. A. Messner & D. F. Sabo (Eds.), *Sport, men, and the gender order: Critical feminist perspectives* (pp. 1-16). Champaign, IL: Human Kinetics.

Minkowitz, D. (1995, November-December). In the name of the father. *Ms.*, pp. 64-71.

Mirandé, A. (1982). Machismo: Rucas, chingasos y chagaderas. *De Colores: Journal of Chicano Expression and Thought* 6(1/2).

Moore, R., & Gillette, D. (1991). *King, warrior, magician, lover: Rediscovering the archetypes of the mature masculine.* New York: Harper Collins.

Moynihan, D. P. (1965). *The negro family: The case for national action.* Washington, DC: U.S. Department of Labor.

Nardi, P. (1994, April). *Do ask and do tell: Stonewalling men's studies.* Paper presented at the annual meeting of the Pacific Sociological Association, San Diego, CA.

Nardi, P. M., Sanders, D., & Marmor, J. (1994). *Growing up before Stonewall: Life stories of some gay men.* New York: Routledge.

Nichols, J. (1975). *Men's liberation: A new definition of masculinity.* New York: Penguin.

Nichols, J. (1977). Butcher than thou: Beyond machismo. In M. P. Levine (Ed.), *Gay men: The sociology of male homosexuality* (pp. 328-342). New York: Harper & Row.

NOMAS. (1995). Statement of principles. In M. S. Kimmel & M. A. Messner (Eds.), *Men's lives* (3rd ed., p. 529). Boston: Allyn & Bacon.

Nonn, T. (1995). Hitting bottom: Homelessness, poverty, and masculinity. In M. S. Kimmel & M. A. Messner (Eds.), *Men's lives* (3rd ed., pp. 225-234). Boston: Allyn & Bacon.

Panghorn, K. (1985). The murdered husband: Family violence and women's lib. In F. Baumli (Ed.), *Men freeing men: Exploding the myth of the traditional male* (pp. 213-215). Jersey City, NJ: New Atlantis.

Paredes, A. (1966). The Anglo-American in Mexican folklore. In R. B. Browne & D. H. Wenkelman (Eds.), *New voices in American studies.* Lafayette, IN: Purdue University Press.

Peña, M. (1991). Class, gender and machismo: The "treacherous woman" folklore of Mexican male workers. *Gender & Society, 5*, 30-46.

Peterson, J. L. (1992). Black men and their same-sex desires and behaviors. In G. Herdt (Ed.), *Gay culture in America: Essays from the field* (pp. 147-164). Boston: Beacon.

Pierce, C. M., & Profit, W. E. (1994). Racial group dynamics: Implications for rearing black males. In R. G. Majors & J. U. Gordon (Eds.), *The American black male* (pp. 167-177). Chicago: Nelson-Hall.

Pleck, J. H. (1976). The male sex role: Definitions, problems, and sources of change. *Journal of Social Issues, 32*, 155-164.

Pleck, J. H. (1982). *The myth of masculinity.* Cambridge: MIT Press.

Pleck, J. H. (1995). Men's power with women, other men, and in society: A men's movement analysis. In M. S. Kimmel & M. A. Messner (Eds.), *Men's lives* (3rd ed., pp. 5-12). Boston: Allyn & Bacon.

Pleck, J. H., & Sawyer, J. (Eds.). (1974). *Men and masculinity.* Englewood Cliffs, NJ: Prentice Hall.

Plummer, K. (1995). *Telling stories: Power, change and social worlds.* New York: Routledge.

Reskin, B. F., & Padavic, I. (1994). *Women and men at work.* Thousand Oaks, CA: Pine Forge.

Reskin, B. F., & Roos, P. A. (1990). *Job queues, gender queues: Explaining women's inroads into male occupations.* Philadelphia: Temple University Press.

Rose, S. D. (1987). Women warriors: The negotiation of gender in a charismatic community. *Sociological Analysis, 48,* 245-258.

Russell, G. (1983). *The changing role of fathers.* London: University of Queensland.

Sabo, D. F. (1994a). Different stakes: Men's pursuit of gender equity in sports. In M. A. Messner & D. F. Sabo (Ed.), *Sex, violence, and power in sports: Rethinking masculinity* (pp. 202-213). Freedom, CA: Crossing Press.

Sabo, D. F. (1994b). Pigskin, patriarchy, and pain. In M. A. Messner & D. F. Sabo (Ed.), *Sex, violence, and power in sports: Rethinking masculinity* (pp. 82-88). Freedom, CA: Crossing Press.

Sabo, D. F. (1995). Caring for men. In J. M. Cookfair (Ed.), *Nursing care in the community* (2nd ed., pp. 346-365). St. Louis: C. V. Mosby.

Sabo, D., & Gordon, D. F. (Eds.). (1995). *Men's health and illness: Gender, power, and the body.* Thousand Oaks, CA: Sage.

Sahagun, L. (1995, July 6). Christian men's movement taps into identity crisis. *Los Angeles Times,* p. A1.

Sanday, P. (1981). *Female power and male dominance: On the origins of sexual inequality.* New York: Cambridge University Press.

Sattel, J. (1976). The inexpressive male: Tragedy or sexual politics? *Social Problems, 23,* 469-477.

Saunders, D. G. (1988). Other "truths" about domestic violence: A reply to McNeely and Robinson-Simpson. *Social Work, 32,* 179-183.

Sawyer, J. (1970, March). *The male liberation movement.* Workshop conducted at the Women's Liberation Teach-in, Northwestern University, Evanston, IL.

Schlafly, P. (1981). How to clean up American by stopping the Equal Rights Amendment. In J. Falwell (Ed.), *How you can help clean up America* (pp. 23-29). Washington, DC: Moral Majority.

Schwalbe, M. (1995a). Mythopoetic men's work as a search for communitas. In M. S. Kimmel & M. A. Messner (Eds.), *Men's lives* (3rd ed., pp. 507-519). Boston: Allyn & Bacon.

Schwalbe, M. (1995b). Why mythopoetic men don't flock to NOMAS. In M. S. Kimmel (Ed.), *The politics of manhood: Profeminist men respond to the mythopoetic men's movement (and the mythopoetic leaders answer)* (pp. 323-332). Philadelphia: Temple University Press.

Schwalbe, M. (1996). *Unlocking the iron cage: The men's movement, gender politics, and American culture.* Oxford, UK: Oxford University Press.

Schwartz, M. D. (1987). Gender and injury in spousal assaults. *Sociological Focus, 20,* 61-75.

Sealander, J., & Smith, D. (1986). The rise and fall of feminist organizations in the 1970's: Dayton as a case study. *Feminist Studies, 12,* 321-341.

Segal, L. (1987). *Is the future female? Troubled thoughts on contemporary feminism.* New York: Peter Bedrick.

Segal, L. (1990). *Slow motion: Changing masculinities, changing men.* New Brunswick, NJ: Rutgers University Press.

Segal, L. (1994). *Straight sex: Rethinking the politics of pleasure.* Berkeley: University of California Press.

Shelton, B. A., & John, D. (1993). Ethnicity, race, and difference: A comparison of white, black, and Hispanic men's household labor time. In J. C. Hood (Ed.), *Men, work, and family* (pp. 131-150). Newbury Park, CA: Sage.

Shiffman, M. (1987). The men's movement: An exploratory empirical investigation. In M. S. Kimmel (Ed.), *Changing men: New directions in research on men and masculinity* (pp. 295-314). Newbury Park, CA: Sage.

Sidel, R. (1986). *Women and children last: The plight of poor women in affluent America.* New York: Penguin.

Sidel, R. (1990). *On her own: Growing up in the shadow of the American dream.* New York: Viking.

Silverstein, M. (1977). The history of a short, unsuccessful academic career. In J. Snodgrass (Ed.), *For men against sexism* (pp. 177-196). Albion, CA: Times Change Press.

Snitow, A., Stansell, C., & Thompson, S. (Eds.). (1983). *Powers of desire: The politics of sexuality.* New York: Monthly Review Press.

Snodgrass, J. (Ed.). (1977). *For men against sexism.* Albion, CA: Times Change Press.

Soares, J. V. (1979). Black and gay. In M. P. Levine (Ed.), *Gay men: The sociology of male homosexuality* (pp. 263-274). New York: Harper & Row.

Stacey, J. (1983). *Patriarchy and socialist revolution in China.* Berkeley: University of California Press.

Stacey, J. (1990). *Brave new families: Stories of domestic upheaval in late twentieth century America.* New York: Basic Books.

Stacey, J., & Gerard, S. E. (1989). "We are not doormats": The influence of feminism on contemporary evangelicalism in the United States. In F. Ginsberg & A. Tsing (Eds.), *Uncertain terms: Negotiating gender in American culture* (pp. 98-117). Boston: Beacon.

Stacey, J., & Thorne, B. (1985). The missing feminist revolution in sociology. *Social Problems, 32,* 301-316.

Staples, R. (1982). *Black masculinity: The black male's role in American society.* San Francisco: Black Scholar Press.

Staples, R. (1986). Black male sexuality. *Changing Men, 17,* 4-6.

Staples, R. (1995a). Health among Afro-American males. In D. Sabo & D. F. Gordon (Eds.), *Men's health and illness: Gender, power, and the body* (pp. 212-138). Thousand Oaks, CA: Sage.

Staples, R. (1995b). Stereotypes of black masculinity: The facts behind the myths. In M. S. Kimmel & M. A. Messner (Eds.), *Men's lives* (3rd ed., pp. 375-380). Boston: Allyn & Bacon.

Steinem, G. (1992). Foreword. In K. L. Hagan (Ed.), *Women respond to the men's movement* (pp. v-ix). San Francisco: Pandora.

Stillion, J. M. (1995). Premature death among males: Extending the bottom line of men's health. In D. Sabo & D. F. Gordon (Eds.), *Men's health and illness: Gender, power, and the body* (pp. 46-67). Thousand Oaks, CA: Sage.

Stoltenberg, J. (1977). Toward gender justice. In J. Snodgrass (Ed.), *For men against sexism* (pp. 74-83). Albion, CA: Times Change Press.

Stoltenberg, J. (1988, Spring/Summer). Gays and the pornography movement: Having the hots for sex discrimination. *Changing Men: Issues in Gender, Sex, and Politics, 19,* 11-13.

Stoltenberg, J. (1989). *Refusing to be a man: Essays on sex and justice.* Portland, OR: Breitenbush.

Stoltenberg, J. (1995, Spring). Whose God is it anyway? Male virgins, blood covenants, and family values. *On the Issues,* pp. 25-29, 51-52.

Straton, J. C. (1994). The myth of the "battered husband syndrome." *Masculinities, 2,* 79-82.

Takagi, D. Y. (1996). Maiden voyage: Excursion into sexuality and identity politics in Asian America. In R. Leong (Ed.), *Asian American sexualities: Dimensions of the gay and lesbian experience* (pp. 21-35). New York: Routledge.

Taylor, R. L. (1994). Black males and social policy: Breaking the cycle of disadvantage. In R. G. Majors & J. U. Gordon (Eds.), *The American black male* (pp. 147-166). Chicago: Nelson-Hall.

Tolson, A. (1977). *The limits of masculinity: Male identity and women's liberation.* New York: Harper & Row.

Tucker, S. (1990). Radical feminism and gay male porn. In M. S. Kimmel (Ed.), *Men confront pornography* (pp. 263-276). New York: Crown.

Waldron, I. (1995). Contributions of changing gender differences in behavior and social roles to changing gender differences in mortality. In D. Sabo & D. F. Gordon (Eds.), *Men's health and illness: Gender, power, and the body* (pp. 22-45). Thousand Oaks, CA: Sage.

Wallace, M. (1978). *Black macho and the myth of the super-woman.* New York: Warner.

Weinstein, J. (1990). What porn did. In M. S. Kimmel (Ed.), *Men confront pornography* (pp. 277-280). New York: Crown.

West, C. (1993). *Race matters.* Boston: Beacon.

Weston, K. (1991). *Families we choose: Lesbians, gays, kinship.* New York: Columbia University Press.

Williams, C. L. (Ed.). (1993). *Doing "women's work": Men in nontraditional occupations.* Newbury Park, CA: Sage.

Williams, W. L. (1986). Gay studies and men's studies. *Journal of the National Association for Women Deans, Administrators, & Counselors, 49,* 38-41.

Willis, E. (1983). Feminism, moralism, and pornography. In A. Snitow, C. Stansell, & S. Thompson (Eds.), *Powers of desire: The politics of sexuality* (pp. 460-467). New York: Monthly Review Press.

Wilson, W. J. (1987). *The truly disadvantaged.* Chicago: University of Chicago Press.

Winter, M. F., & Robert, E. R. (1980). Male dominance, late capitalism, and the growth of instrumental reason. *Berkeley Journal of Sociology, 25,* 249-280.

Wittberg, P. (1989). Feminist consciousness among American nuns: Patterns of ideological diffusion. *Women's Studies International Forum, 12,* 529-537.

Wittig, M. (1992). *The straight mind and other essays.* Boston: Beacon.

Wittman, C. (1970). Refugees from Amerika: A gay manifesto. In K. Jay & A. Young (Eds.), *Out of the closets: Voices of gay liberation* (pp. 330-345). New York: Douglas.

About the Author

Michael A. Messner is Associate Professor in the Department of Sociology and the Program for the Study of Women and Men in Society at the University of Southern California, where he teaches courses on sex and gender, men and masculinity, sexuality, and gender and sport. He is coeditor of *Men's Lives* (1995) and *Sport, Men, and the Gender Order: Critical Feminist Perspectives* (1990). He authored *Power at Play: Sports and the Problem of Masculinity* (1992) and coauthored *Sex, Violence, and Power in Sports: Rethinking Masculinity* (1994). He is a member of the National Organization for Men Against Sexism (NOMAS) and has worked for more than a decade as a contributing editor for *Changing Men*, a pro-feminist magazine. He received his Ph.D. in sociology at the University of California at Berkeley.